# THE HOME VEGETABLE GARDEN

THE CLASSIC USDA FARMERS' BULLETIN NO. 255
WITH TIPS AND TRADITIONAL METHODS
IN SUSTAINABLE GARDENING AND PERMACULTURE

BY **U.S. DEPARTMENT OF AGRICULTURE**

ORIGINALLY PUBLISHED IN 1906

**LEGACY EDITION**
CLASSIC FARMERS BULLETIN LIBRARY
BOOK NO. 255

Doublebit Press
Eugene, OR

*New content, introduction, and annotations*
*Copyright © 2020 by Doublebit Press. All rights reserved.*

*Doublebit Press is an imprint of Eagle Nest Press*
*www.doublebitpress.com | Eugene, OR, USA*

*Original content under the public domain. Originally published in 1906 by the U.S. Department of Agriculture.*

*This title, along with other Doublebit Press books including the Classic Farmers Bulletin Library, are available at a volume discount for youth groups, outdoors clubs, or reading groups.*

*Doublebit Press Legacy Edition ISBN*
*Paperback: 978-1-64389-132-3*

*Disclaimer: Because of its age and historic context, this book could contain content on present-day inappropriate methods, activities, outdated medical information, unsafe chemical and mechanical processes, or culturally and racially insensitive content. Doublebit Press, or its employees, authors, and other affiliates, assume no liability for any actions performed by readers or any damages that might be related to information contained in this book. This text has been published for historical study and for personal literary enrichment toward the goal of preserving the American handcraft tradition, timeless trade skills, and traditional artisanal knowledge.*

*First Doublebit Press Legacy Edition Printing, 2020*

*Printed in the United States of America when purchased at retail in the USA*

# INTRODUCTION
## Classic Farmers Bulletin Library

The old experts of artisanal trades, country and homestead knowledge, and the woods and mountains taught timeless principles and skills for centuries. Through their timeless books, the old experts offered rich descriptions of how the world works and encouraged learning through personal experiences *by doing*. Over the last 125 years, manufacturing, farming, and construction have substantially changed. Of course, many things have gotten simpler as equipment and technology have improved. In addition, some activities of pre-digital times are now no longer in vogue, or are even outright considered inappropriate or illegal. However, despite many of the positive changes in manufacturing and crafting methods that have occurred over the years, *there are many other skills and much knowledge that have been forgotten.*

By publishing the reprint series of the old USDA *Farmers' Bulletin*, it is our goal at Doublebit Press to do what we can to preserve and share the works from forgotten teachers that form the cornerstone of the history of the American artisans and traditional crafts. So much farm, homestead, and handcraft knowledge was passed to each generation through experience and hard work. An original mission of the US Department of Agriculture was to optimize farm outputs and increase the quality of life on farms through handcrafts, construction, and old-time farm tricks, tips, and skills. In their *Farmers' Bulletin* series, the USDA captured and passed on knowledge that applied to far more than just farmers!

Through remastered reprint editions of timeless classics, perhaps we can regain some of this lost knowledge for future generations. Today's interest in mastery of old handcraft skills, homestead self-sufficiency, and artisanal character has renewed an interest in the old arts. Luckily, the USDA's *Farmers' Bulletin* series contains thousands of pamphlets dedicated to teaching, improving life, and ensuring self-sufficiency to thrive in both the city and on a farm.

This book is an important contribution traditional handcraft and country skills literature and has important historical and collector value toward preserving the American handcraft and outdoors tradition. The knowledge it holds is an invaluable reference for practicing skills and hand craft methods. Its chapters thoroughly discuss some of the essential building blocks of knowledge that are fundamental but may have been forgotten as equipment gets fancier and technology gets smarter. In short, this reprint of the *Farmers' Bulletin* pamphlets was chosen for Legacy Edition printing because much of the basic skills and knowledge it contains has been forgotten or put to the wayside in trade for more modern conveniences and methods.

With technology playing a major role in everyday life, sometimes we need to take a step back in time to find those basic building blocks used for gaining mastery – the things that we have luckily not completely lost and has been recorded in books over the last two centuries. These skills aren't forgotten, they've just been shelved. *It's time to unshelve them once again and reclaim the lost knowledge of self-sufficiency.*

Based on this commitment to preserving our outdoors and handcraft artisanal heritage, we have taken great pride in publishing this book as a complete original work. We hope it is worthy of both study and collection by outdoors folk in the modern era of outdoors and traditional skills life.

Unlike many other photocopy reproductions of classic books that are common on the market, this Legacy Edition does not simply place poor photography of old texts on our pages and use error-prone optical scanning or computer-generated text. We want our work to speak for itself, and reflect the quality demanded by our customers who spend their hard-earned money. With this in mind, each Legacy Edition book that has been chosen for publication is carefully remastered from original print books, *with the Doublebit Legacy Edition printed and laid out in the exact way that it was presented at its original publication.* We provide a beautiful, memorable experience that is as true to the original text as best as possible, but with the aid of modern technology to make as beautiful a reading experience as possible for books that can be over a century old.

Because of its age and because it is presented in its original form, the book may contain misspellings, inking errors from print plates, and other printing blemishes that were common for the age. However, these are exactly the things that we feel give the book its character, which we preserved in this Legacy Edition. During digitization, we ensured that each illustration in the text was clean and sharp with the least amount of loss from being copied and digitized as possible. Full-page plate illustrations are presented as they were found, often including the extra blank page that was often behind a plate. For the covers, we use the original cover design to give the book its original feel. We are sure you'll appreciate the fine touches and attention to detail that your Legacy Edition has to offer.

For traditional handcrafters and classic artisanal enthusiasts who demand the best from their equipment, this Doublebit Press Legacy Edition reprint was made with you in mind. Both important and minor details have equally both been accounted for by our publishing staff, down to the cover, font, layout, and images. It is the goal of Doublebit Legacy Edition series to be worthy of collection in any outdoorsperson's library and that can be passed to future generations.

Every book selected to be in this series offers unique views and instruction on important skills, advice, tips, tidbits, anecdotes, stories, and experiences that will enrich the repertoire of any person who enjoys escaping a bit from today's modern technology-based, cookie-cutter, and highly industrialized skills. Instead, folks seeking to make things with their hands like the old days may find great value from these resurrected instructional manuals from the past. These books were not simply written to be shelved in a library – they contain our history and forgotten methods to make things with real character and energy with a *human* component.

Therefore, to learn the most basic building blocks of a craft leads to mastery of all its aspects. We hope this book helps you along this path with its rich descriptions and illustrations!

**About the USDA Farmers' Bulletin Series**

Back in the early 1900s, the US Department of Agriculture (USDA) began publication of small pamphlets that were meant to improve the outputs of America's farms, promote self-sufficiency, and help farmers and farming communities thrive. This publication series continued for decades, and volumes were always available when someone wanted to learn more about a specific skill or topic that could come in handy on the homestead.

Each of the 2,000+ volumes specializes in one specific topic, be it growing a certain crop, raising a particular animal, or building a type of farm structure. Each of the pamphlets captured the best knowledge available at that time, which often represented decades or centuries of old farmer knowledge, which we know, is incredibly useful and reliable!

As we continue to blaze paths into the digital frontier, many of these lost "farmers' tips" have become more useful than ever, particularly to folks looking to start homesteads and small-scale farms, as well as those who just want to live more sustainably, simply, and consciously in light of today's factory processed world. The *Farmers' Bulletin* is also highly useful for people who live in cities, as they contain much information for community gardens, urban and rooftop farming, and sustainable living tips.

Unfortunately, many of these print volumes of the *Farmers' Bulletin* are now out of print. Indeed, because these texts are in the public domain, they are easily found and are available on the Internet. However, many of these books that are easily found on the web are often low-resolution photocopies, complete with scribble marks or other distracting spots. For the first time, high-quality, professionally restored *Farmers' Bulletin* reissues are being made by Doublebit Press to increase access to the timeless knowledge that each contains.

This Doublebit Press Legacy Edition republishes this tradition of handcrafted quality and artisanal work. We hope that this deluxe printed edition of this book will help you gain mastery in your craft, as it is presented in the exact form that it was originally published. Even today, the knowledge contained within its pages are timeless and have much to teach!

Finally, as works of art, the USDA *Farmers' Bulletin* issues contain beautiful illustrations and line art that are a sign of simpler, yet authentic times when quality mattered and craftsmanship was king. This collectible volume makes a great addition to the bookshelf of any handcrafter, maker, artisan, farmer, homesteader, or outdoors enthusiast!

Enjoy some old-time, vintage charm when the government actually encouraged you to be self-sufficient with these beautifully illustrated and classic instruction manuals by the USDA!

U. S. DEPARTMENT OF AGRICULTURE.

FARMERS' BULLETIN No. 255.

# THE HOME VEGETABLE GARDEN.

BY

W. R. BEATTIE,
*Assistant Horticulturist, Bureau of Plant Industry.*

WASHINGTON:
GOVERNMENT PRINTING OFFICE.
1906.

## LETTER OF TRANSMITTAL.

U. S. DEPARTMENT OF AGRICULTURE,
BUREAU OF PLANT INDUSTRY,
OFFICE OF THE CHIEF,
*Washington, D. C., April 12, 1906.*

SIR: I have the honor to transmit and to recommend for publication as a Farmers' Bulletin the accompanying paper on "The Home Vegetable Garden," prepared by Mr. W. R. Beattie, Assistant Horticulturist.

This bulletin supersedes Farmers' Bulletin No. 94, "The Vegetable Garden."

Respectfully,
B. T. GALLOWAY,
*Chief of Bureau.*

Hon. JAMES WILSON,
*Secretary of Agriculture.*

## CONTENTS.

|  | Page. |
|---|---|
| Introduction | 5 |
| Location of the garden | 6 |
| Plan and arrangement of the garden | 6 |
|     Kind of cultivation to be employed | 8 |
|     Location of crops | 8 |
|     Succession of crops | 9 |
| Preparation of the soil | 9 |
|     Drainage | 9 |
|     Plowing | 9 |
|     Smoothing and pulverizing the soil | 10 |
|     Special preparation | 10 |
| Fertilizers | 11 |
|     Barnyard manure | 11 |
|     Commercial fertilizers | 11 |
| Seeds and plants for the garden | 12 |
|     Early plants in hotbeds | 12 |
|     Early plants in cold frames | 15 |
| The seed bed | 15 |
|     Seed sowing | 15 |
|     Care of the seed bed | 16 |
| The handling of plants | 16 |
|     Hardening off | 16 |
|     Importance of thinning | 17 |
|     Effects of transplanting | 17 |
|     Special methods of transplanting | 18 |
|     Setting in the open ground | 18 |
| Time of planting | 19 |
| Protection of plants | 19 |
|     Protection from heat | 20 |
|     Protection from cold | 20 |
| Cultivation of garden crops | 21 |
|     Tools for use in the garden | 21 |
| Irrigation of garden crops | 22 |
| Precautions to avoid attacks of insects and diseases | 23 |
| Cultural hints for garden crops | 24 |
|     Artichoke (Globe), artichoke (Jerusalem), asparagus | 24 |
|     Beans, beets, Brussels sprouts | 26, 27 |
|     Cabbage, cardoon, carrot, cauliflower, celeriac, celery, chervil, chicory, chive, citron, collards, corn salad, corn (sweet), cress, cucumber | 28–32 |
|     Dandelion | 33 |
|     Eggplant, endive | 33 |
|     Garlic | 34 |
|     Horse-radish | 34 |
|     Kale (or borecole), kohl-rabi | 34 |

| | Page. |
|---|---|
| Cultural hints for garden crops—Continued. | |
|    Leek, lettuce | 35 |
|    Melon—muskmelon; melon—watermelon; mustard | 35, 36 |
|    New Zealand spinach | 36 |
|    Okra (or gumbo), onions | 36, 37 |
|    Parsley, parsnip, peas, peppers, physalis, potato (Irish), potato (sweet), pumpkin | 38–42 |
|    Radish, rhubarb, ruta-baga | 42, 43 |
|    Salsify (or vegetable oyster), spinach, squash | 43, 44 |
|    Tomato, turnip | 44, 45 |
|    Vegetable marrow | 45 |
| Gardener's planting table | 46 |

## ILLUSTRATIONS.

| | | Page |
|---|---|---|
| Fig. | 1. Plan of a half-acre garden | 7 |
| | 2. Plan of a city-lot or back-yard garden | 8 |
| | 3. Cross section of land bedded up for early crops | 10 |
| | 4. Cross section of land ridged up for early crops | 10 |
| | 5. Cross section of land showing trenches employed in the cultivation of celery and similar crops | 11 |
| | 6. Flat, or tray, for starting plants or transplanting | 12 |
| | 7. Hotbed, showing frame and sash | 13 |
| | 8. Cross section of temporary hotbed | 13 |
| | 9. Cross section of permanent hotbed | 13 |
| | 10. Cross section of pipe-heated hotbed | 14 |
| | 11. Cross section of permanent hotbed with enlarged pit | 14 |
| | 12. Celery plants, showing effect of transplanting on root system | 17 |
| | 13. Berry box used for starting and transplanting early plants | 18 |
| | 14. Cross section of land illustrating the use of the dibble in setting plants | 19 |
| | 15. Board used for protection of plants | 20 |
| | 16. Small-tooth horse cultivator | 21 |
| | 17. Spading fork | 21 |
| | 18. Dibbles used for transplanting | 21 |
| | 19. Transplanting trowel | 22 |
| | 20. Onion hoe | 22 |
| | 21. Hand weeder | 22 |
| | 22. Thinning or weeding hook | 22 |
| | 23. Wheel hoe | 22 |
| | 24. Cross section of soil showing arrangement of tiles for subirrigation | 23 |
| | 25. Globe or bur artichoke | 24 |
| | 26. Asparagus plant | 25 |
| | 27. Chive | 31 |
| | 28. Device for protecting young cucumber plants | 32 |
| | 29. Kohl-rabi | 34 |
| | 30. Onions | 37 |
| | 31. Cross section of Potato or Multiplier onion | 37 |
| | 32. Top or Tree onion, producing bulblets on top of stem | 37 |
| | 33. Parsnips | 38 |
| | 34. Spinach plant in proper condition for cutting | 44 |

B. P. I.—211.

# THE HOME VEGETABLE GARDEN.

## INTRODUCTION.

Perhaps the most characteristic feature of our northern and eastern farms is the home vegetable garden. Even where no orchard has been planted, and where the ornamental surroundings of the home have been neglected, a fairly well-kept garden in which are grown a number of the staple kinds of vegetables is generally to be found. In many cases the principal interest in the garden is manifested by the women of the household and much of the necessary care is given by them. A small portion of the garden inclosure is generally devoted to the cultivation of flowers, and a number of medicinal plants are invariably present. Throughout the newer parts of the country one finds that the conditions governing the maintenance and use of the vegetable garden are somewhat different, and, while a number of vegetable crops may be grown somewhere on the farm, there is wanting that distinction so characteristic of the typical New England kitchen garden.

It would be impossible to make an accurate estimate of the value of crops grown in the kitchen gardens of the United States, but from careful observation the statement can safely be made that a well-kept garden will yield a return ten to fifteen times greater than would the same area and location if devoted to general farm crops. A half acre devoted to the various kinds of garden crops will easily supply a family with $100 worth of vegetables during the year, while the average return for farm crops is considerably less than one-tenth of this amount. A bountiful supply of vegetables close at hand where they may be secured at a few moments' notice is of even more importance than the mere money value.

Fresh vegetables from the home garden are not subjected to exposure on the markets or in transportation and are not liable to become infected in any way. Many of the products of the garden lose their characteristic flavor when not used within a few hours after gathering. By means of the home garden the production of the vegetable supply for the family is directly under control, and in many cases is the only way whereby clean, fresh produce may be secured. The home vegetable garden is worthy of increased attention, and a greater number and variety of crops should be included in the garden.

Suggestions are herein given as to the location of the garden, the soil and its preparation, fertilizers, seeds, and plants, with brief cultural methods for a number of the more important crops.

## LOCATION OF THE GARDEN.

The question of the proximity to the house or other buildings is of great importance when locating the garden. In old homesteads the garden was generally located directly adjacent to the house, requiring but a few steps from the kitchen to reach the extreme parts of the garden. The work of caring for a garden is usually done at spare times, and for this reason alone the location should be near the dwelling. In case the site chosen for the garden should become unsuitable for any cause it is not a difficult matter to change the location. Many persons prefer to plant the garden in a different location every five or six years.

The lay of the land has considerable influence upon the time that the soil can be worked, and a gentle slope toward the south or southeast is most desirable for the production of early crops. It is an advantage to have protection on the north and northwest by either a hill, a group of trees, evergreens, a hedge, buildings, a tight board fence, or a stone wall to break the force of the wind.

Good natural drainage of the garden area is of prime importance. The land should have sufficient fall to drain off surplus water during heavy rains, but the fall should not be so great that the soil will be washed. The surface of the garden should not contain depressions in which water will accumulate or stand. Waste water from surrounding land should not flow toward the garden, and the fall below should be such that there will be no danger of flood water backing up. The garden should not be located along the banks of a creek or stream that will be liable to overflow during the growing season.

A good fence around the garden plot is almost indispensable, and it should be a safeguard against all farm animals, including poultry, and should be close enough to keep out rabbits. A tight board fence will accomplish this result and also serve as a wind-break.

## PLAN AND ARRANGEMENT OF THE GARDEN.

It would be difficult to give a plan or specific arrangement for a garden that would suit all demands, and such a plan must be devised by each individual grower. Suggestive arrangements, however, are here presented, with the idea that they can readily be changed to suit local conditions.

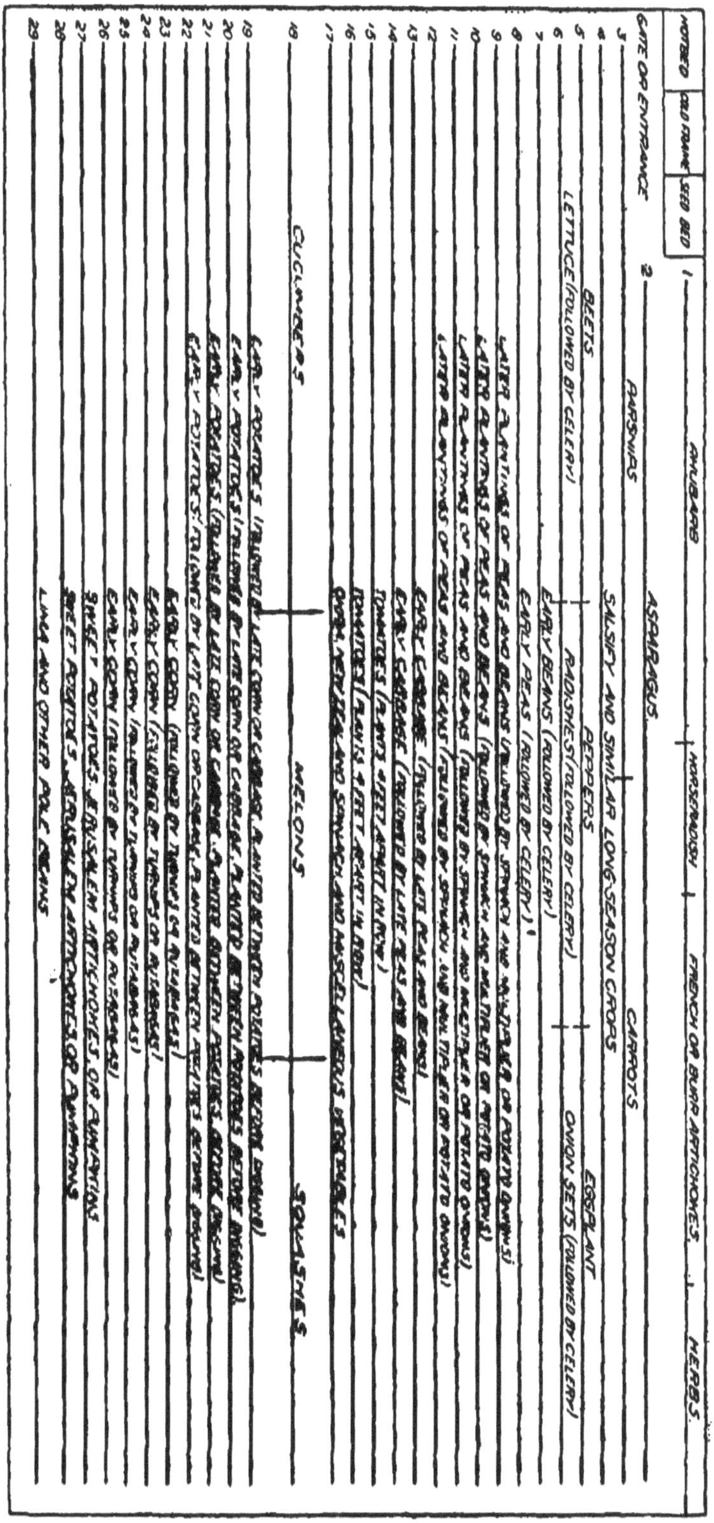

FIG. 1.—Plan of a half-acre garden. Length, 220 feet; width, 100 feet.

## KIND OF CULTIVATION TO BE EMPLOYED.

The first consideration in planning the arrangement of a garden is the kind of cultivation that is to be employed. Where the work is to be done mainly by means of horse tools the arrangement should be such as to give the longest possible rows, and straight outlines should be followed. The garden should be free from paths across the rows, and turning spaces should be provided at the ends. (Fig. 1.) For hand cultivation the arrangement can be quite different, as the garden may be laid off in sections, with transverse walks, and the rows can be much closer for most crops. (Fig. 2.) Horse cultivation is recommended whenever possible, as it very materially lessens the labor and cost of caring for the crops.

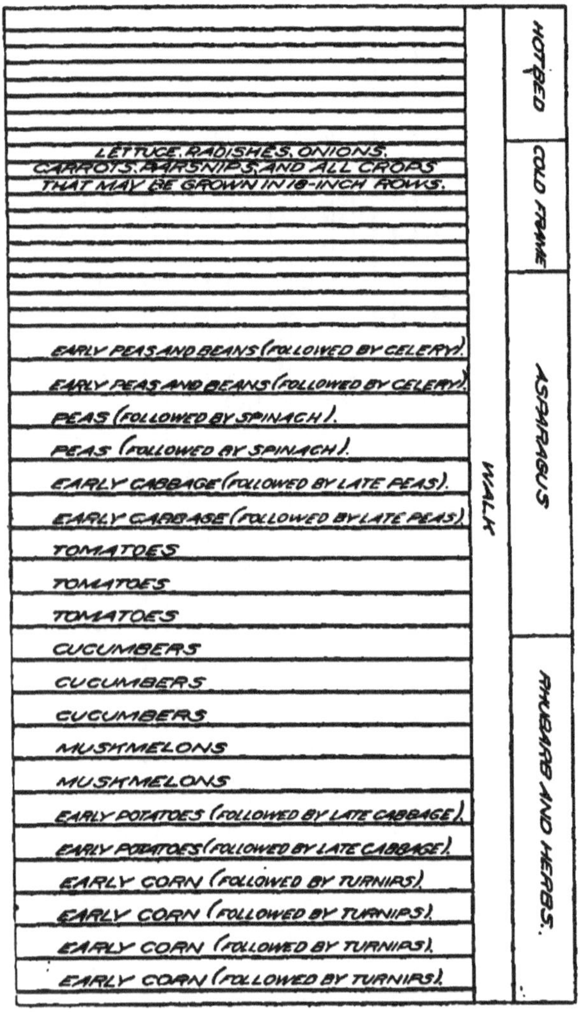

FIG. 2.—Plan of a city-lot or back-yard garden. 50 by 90 feet.

## LOCATION OF CROPS.

The second matter for consideration is the location of permanent crops, such as asparagus and rhubarb, and if any of the small fruits, such as raspberries, currants, and gooseberries, are to be planted within the garden inclosure, they should be included with the permanent crops. The area devoted to the hotbed, cold frame, and seed bed should be decided upon, but these may be shifted more or less from year to year or located in some convenient place outside of the garden.

Where there is any great variation in the composition of the soil in different parts of the garden it will be advisable to take this into consideration when arranging for the location of the various crops. If a part of the land is low and moist, such crops as celery, onions, and late cucumbers should be placed there. If part of the soil is high, warm, and dry, that is the proper location for early crops and those that need quick, warm soil.

### SUCCESSION OF CROPS.

In planning the location of the various crops in the garden, due consideration should be given to the matter of succession in order that the land may be occupied at all times. As a rule it would not be best to have a second planting of the same crop follow the first, but some such arrangement as early peas followed by celery, or early cabbage or potatoes followed by late beans or corn, and similar combinations, are more satisfactory. In the South as many as three crops may be grown one after the other on the same land, but at the extreme north, where the season is short, but one crop can be grown, or possibly two by some such combination as early peas followed by turnips.

### PREPARATION OF THE SOIL.

Where there is considerable choice in the location of the garden plot, it is often possible to select land that will require very little special preparation. On the other hand, it may be necessary to take an undesirable soil and bring it into suitable condition, and it is generally surprising to note the change that can be wrought in a single season.

### DRAINAGE.

There are very few soils that are not improved by some form of drainage. Heavy clay soils are benefited most by drainage, but sandy soils having a clay subsoil are made warmer and greatly improved by having the excess soil water removed quickly.

### PLOWING.

Autumn is the time for plowing hard or stiff clay soils, especially if in a part of the country where freezing takes place, as the action of the frost during the winter will break the soil into fine particles and render it suitable for planting. Sandy loams and soils that contain a large amount of humus may be plowed in the spring, but the work should be done early in order that the soil may settle before planting. In the Southern States, where there is not sufficient frost to mellow the soil, this process must be accomplished by means of frequent cultivations, in order that the air may act upon the soil particles. It is desirable to plow the garden early, at least a few days sooner than for general field crops.

Sandy soils will bear plowing much earlier than heavy clay soils. The usual test is to squeeze together a handful, and if the soil adheres in a ball it is too wet for working. In the garden greater depth of plowing should be practiced than for ordinary farm crops, as the roots of many of the vegetables go deeply into the soil. Subsoiling will be found advantageous in most cases, as the drainage and general movement of the soil moisture will be improved thereby.

Hand spading should be resorted to only in very small gardens or where it is desirable to prepare a small area very thoroughly.

### SMOOTHING AND PULVERIZING THE SOIL.

After plowing, the next important step is to smooth and pulverize the soil. If the soil be well prepared before planting, the work of caring for the crops will be very materially lessened. It is not sufficient that the land be smooth and fine on top, but the pulverizing process should extend as deep as the plowing. Some gardeners prefer to thoroughly cut the land with a disk harrow before plowing, so that when it is turned by the plow the bottom soil will be fine and mellow. After the plow the disk or cutting harrow is again brought into play and the pulverizing process completed. If the soil is a trifle too dry and contains lumps, it may be necessary to use some form of roller or clod crusher to bring it down. For smoothing the surface and filling up depressions a float or drag made from planks or scantlings will be found serviceable.

FIG. 3.—Cross section of land bedded up for early crops.

### SPECIAL PREPARATION.

For growing certain crops it has often been found advisable to prepare the ground in a special manner. Such crops as beets, radishes, and onions are sometimes grown on beds 6 to 10 feet in width and raised 6 to 8 inches, with narrow walks between, as shown in figure 3. From Baltimore southward cabbage, cauliflower, and similar crops are frequently grown on top or on the side of ridges. When the plants are set on top of the ridge, better drainage for the roots is secured. When set on the south side

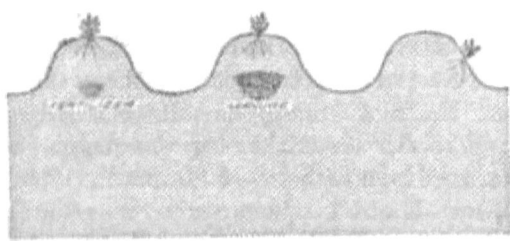

FIG. 4.—Cross section of land ridged up for early crops.

of the ridge, greater warmth and earlier maturity will be secured, and when planted on the north side, the growth is retarded. The ridging method is illustrated by figure 4. For growing celery and a few similar crops it has often been found advisable to place the plants in furrows

FIG. 5.—Cross section of land showing trenches employed in the cultivation of celery and similar crops.

or slight trenches in order that the soil removed may be available for working in around the plants as they mature. (Fig. 5.)

## FERTILIZERS.

The kind of fertilizer employed has a marked influence upon the character and quality of the vegetables produced. For the garden only those fertilizers that have been carefully prepared should be used. Fertilizers of organic composition, such as barnyard manure, should have passed through the fermenting stage before being used. The use of night soil generally is not to be recommended, as its application, unless properly treated for the destruction of disease germs, may prove dangerous to health.

### BARNYARD MANURE.

For garden crops there is no fertilizer that will compare with good, well-rotted barnyard manure. In localities where a supply of such manure can not be secured it will be necessary to depend upon commercial fertilizers, but the results are rarely so satisfactory. In selecting manure for the garden, care should be taken that it does not contain any element that will be injurious to the soil. An excess of sawdust or shavings used as bedding will have a tendency to produce sourness in the soil. Chicken, pigeon, and sheep manures rank high as fertilizers, their value being somewhat greater than ordinary barnyard manures, and almost as great as some of the lower grades of commercial fertilizers. The manure from fowls is especially adapted for dropping in the hills or rows of plants.

### COMMERCIAL FERTILIZERS.

Commercial fertilizers are sold under a guaranteed analysis, and generally at a price consistent with their fertilizing value. No definite rule can be given for the kind or quantity of fertilizer to be applied, as this varies with the crop and the land. At first the only safe procedure is to use a good high-grade fertilizer at the rate of from 1,000 to 2,000 pounds to the acre and note the results. Market gardeners frequently apply as much as 2,500 pounds of high-grade fertilizer per acre each year.

For further information on this subject, see Farmers' Bulletins Nos. 77 on The Liming of Soils, 192 on Barnyard Manure, and 222, Experiment Station Work, XXVIII, which contains a chapter on the Home Mixing of Fertilizers.

## SEEDS AND PLANTS FOR THE GARDEN.

The supply of seeds for the garden should be secured some time in advance of the planting season. During the winter months send for the catalogue of some seedsman in your part of the country and make a selection of the kinds and quantities of seeds that you desire to plant. Garden seeds can frequently be secured of some local dealer who handles them in conjunction with other goods. Many of the garden seeds lose their vitality after one year's time, and old seeds should, as a rule, not be relied upon.

FIG. 6.—Flat, or tray, for starting plants or transplanting.

Throughout the Northern States it is desirable to start plants of certain crops before the danger of frost has passed. The simplest method of starting a limited number of early plants is by means of a shallow box placed in a south window of the dwelling. (Fig. 6.) After the plants appear, the box should be turned each day to prevent the plants drawing toward the light.

## EARLY PLANTS IN HOTBEDS.

The most common method of starting early plants in the North is by means of a hotbed. The hotbed consists of an inclosure covered with sash and supplied with some form of heat, usually fermenting stable manure, to keep the plants warm and in a growing condition. As a rule, the hotbed should not be placed within the garden inclosure, but near some frequently used path or building where it can receive attention without interfering with other work. The hotbed should always face to the south, and the south side of either a dwelling, barn, tight board fence, hedge, or anything affording similar protection, will furnish a good location.

In the North the hotbed should be started in February or early in March, in order that such plants as the tomato and early cabbage may be well grown in time to plant in the open ground. There are two or three forms of hotbeds that are worthy of description, and the plans suggested may be modified to suit local conditions.

A temporary hotbed, such as would ordinarily be employed on the farm, is easily constructed by the use of manure from the horse stable as a means of furnishing the heat. Select a well-drained location,

FIG. 7.—Hotbed, showing frame and sash.

where the bed will be sheltered, shake out the manure into a broad, flat heap, and thoroughly compact it by tramping. The manure heap should be 8 or 9 feet wide, 18 to 24 inches deep when compacted, and of any desired length, according to the number of sash to be employed. The

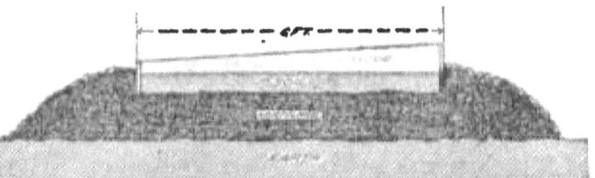

FIG. 8.—Cross section of temporary hotbed.

manure for hotbed purposes should contain sufficient litter, such as leaves or straw, to prevent its packing soggy, and should spring slightly when trodden upon.

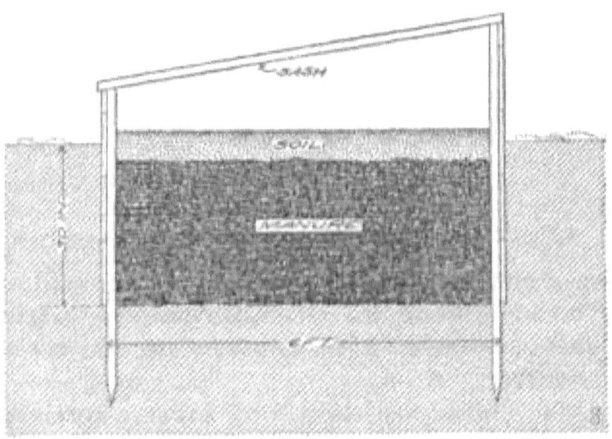

FIG. 9.—Cross section of permanent hotbed.

After the manure has been properly tramped and leveled, the frames to support the sash are placed in position facing toward the south. These frames are generally made to carry 4 standard hotbed sash, and the front board should be 4 to 6 inches lower than the back, in order that water will drain from the glass. When the frame is in position upon the manure, the surface hotbed will appear as shown in figures 7 and 8. Three to five inches of good garden loam or specially prepared soil is spread evenly over the area inclosed by the frame, the sash put on, and the bed allowed to heat. At first the temperature of the bed will run quite high, but no seeds should be planted until the soil temperature falls to 80° F., which will be in about three days.

Hotbeds having more or less permanence may be so constructed as to be heated either with fermenting manure, a stove, a brick flue, or by means of radiating pipes supplied with steam or hot water from a dwelling or other heating plant. For a permanent bed in which fermenting manure is to supply the heat, a pit 24 to 30 inches in depth should be provided. The sides and ends of the pit may be supported by brick walls or by a lining of 2-inch plank held in place by stakes. Figures 9, 10, and 11 illustrate different methods of constructing permanent hotbeds.

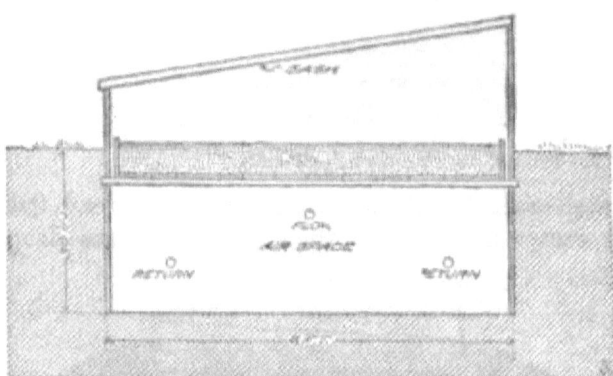

FIG. 10.—Cross section of pipe-heated hotbed.

Standard hotbed sash are 3 by 6 feet in size, and are usually constructed of white pine or cypress. As a rule, hotbed sash can be purchased cheaper than they can be made locally, and are on sale by seedsmen and dealers in garden supplies. In the colder parts of the country, in addition to glazed sash either board shutters, straw mats, burlap, or old carpet will be required as a covering during cold nights. It is also desirable to have a supply of straw or loose manure on hand to throw over the bed in case of extremely cold weather.

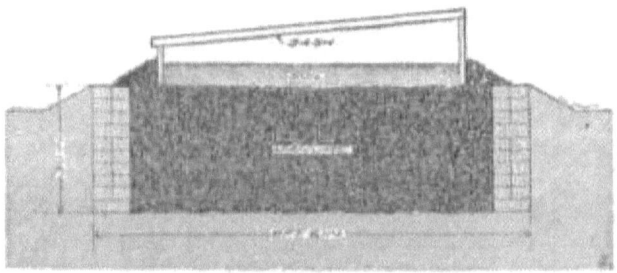

FIG. 11.—Cross section of permanent hotbed with enlarged pit.

During bright days the hotbed will heat very quickly from the sunshine on the glass and it will be necessary to ventilate during the early morning by slightly raising the sash on the opposite side from the wind. Care should be taken in ventilating to protect the plants from a draft of cold air. Toward evening the sash should be closed in order that the bed may become sufficiently warm before nightfall.

Hotbeds should be watered on bright days and in the morning only. Watering in the evening or on cloudy days will have a tendency to chill the bed and increase the danger from freezing. After watering, the bed should be well ventilated to dry the foliage of the plants and the surface of the soil, to prevent the plants being lost by damping-off fungus or mildew.

### EARLY PLANTS IN COLD FRAMES.

The construction of cold frames is the same as for temporary hotbeds except that no manure or other heating material is provided. The frames used are similar to those shown in figure 7. Cold frames are covered by means of ordinary hotbed sash, or cotton cloth may be substituted for the sash. In the North the use of the cold frame is for hardening off plants that have been started in the hotbed, preparatory to setting them in the garden. In the South, where the weather is not so severe, the cold frame is made to take the place of the hotbed in starting early plants. The same methods of handling recommended for a hotbed should apply to a cold frame, and thorough ventilation should be maintained.

### THE SEED BED.

In the broadest sense the entire garden is a seed bed, as the seeds of many of the crops are planted where they are to grow. As the term "seed bed" is used here it refers to some specially prepared place for starting plants, from which they may be transplanted to their permanent positions in the garden. The location of an outdoor seed bed should be such that it may be conveniently reached for watering, and it should be naturally protected from drying winds.

Good soil for a seed bed consists of one part of well-rotted manure, two parts of good garden loam or rotted sods, and one part of sharp, fine sand. The manure should be thoroughly rotted, but it should not have been exposed to the weather and the strength leached out of it. The addition of leaf mold or peat will tend to make the soil better adapted for seed-bed purposes. Mix all the ingredients together in a heap, stirring well with a shovel, after which the soil should be sifted and placed in boxes or in the bed ready for sowing the seed.

Weed seeds and the spores of fungous diseases that are present in the soil for a seed bed may be killed by placing the soil in pans and baking it for an hour in a hot oven.

### SEED SOWING.

Garden seeds should always be sown in straight rows regardless of where the planting is made. If a window box is employed for starting early plants in a dwelling, the soil should be well firmed and then laid off in straight rows about 2 inches apart. The same method holds good for planting seeds in a hotbed, cold frame, or bed in the garden, except that the rows should be farther apart than in the window box. By planting in straight rows the seedlings will be more uniform in size and shape, and thinning and cultivating will be more easily accomplished. In all cases where the soil of the seed bed is not too wet it should be well firmed or pressed down before laying off and marking for sowing the seeds. After the seeds are sown and covered, the surface should again be firmed by means of a smooth board.

No definite rule can be given for the depth to which seeds should be planted, for the depth should vary with the kind of seed and with the character and condition of the soil. In heavy clay and moist soils the covering should be lighter than in sandy or dry soils. In all cases the depth should be uniform, and when planting seeds in boxes or a bed the grooves in which the seeds are planted should be made with the edge of a thin lath.

### CARE OF THE SEED BED.

The seed bed should never be allowed to become dry, but great care should be taken that too much water is not applied. Plants require the action of air upon their roots and an excess of water in the soil will exclude the air. Too frequent and heavy waterings will cause the damping-off of the seedlings.

### THE HANDLING OF PLANTS.

Successful transplanting of indoor-grown plants to the garden or field depends largely upon their proper treatment during the two weeks preceding the time of their removal. Spindling and tender plants will not withstand the exposure of the open ground so well as sturdy, well-grown plants, such as may be secured by proper handling.

### HARDENING OFF.

Plants grown in a house, hotbed, or cold frame will require to be hardened off before planting in the garden. By the process of hardening off, the plants are gradually acclimated to the effects of the sun and wind so that they will stand transplanting to the open ground. Hardening off is usually accomplished by ventilating freely and by reducing the amount of water applied to the plant bed. The plant bed should not become so dry that the plants will wilt or be seriously checked in their growth. After a few days it will be possible to leave the plants uncovered during the entire day and on mild nights. By the time the plants are required for setting in the garden they should be thoroughly acclimated to outdoor conditions and can be transplanted with but few losses.

## IMPORTANCE OF THINNING.

Where plants are not to be transplanted twice, but remain in the plant bed until required for setting in the garden, it may be necessary to thin them somewhat. This part of the work should be done as soon as the plants are large enough to pull, and before they begin to "draw" or become spindling from crowding.

When thinning plants in the plant bed it should be the aim to remove the centers of the thick bunches, leaving the spaces as uniform as possible. When thinning the rows of seedlings in the garden the best plants should be allowed to remain, but due consideration should be given to the matter of proper spacing. Failure to thin plants properly will invariably result in the production of an inferior crop.

## EFFECTS OF TRANSPLANTING.

Fig. 12.—Celery plants, showing effect of transplanting on root system.

At the North, where the growing season is short, it is necessary to transplant several of the garden crops in order to secure strong plants that will mature within the limits of the growing season. In the Southern States the season is longer, and transplanting, while desirable, may not be necessary, as many crops that must be started indoors at the North can be planted in the garden where they are to remain. Transplanting should be done as soon as the seedlings are large enough to handle, and again when the plants begin to crowd one another.

Aside from producing more uniform and hardy plants, the transplanting process has several other very marked influences. Certain crops which are grown for their straight roots are often injured by having their roots bent or broken in transplanting. On the other hand, such plants as celery, which at first have a straight root and are grown for their tops, are greatly benefited by transplanting. Figure 12 shows two celery plants from the same seeding, the one on the left having been transplanted and the one on the right allowed to remain in the seed bed until time for planting in the garden. In all cases transplanting has a tendency to increase the number of small roots, and these are the main dependence of the plant at the time it is set in the open ground.

## SPECIAL METHODS OF TRANSPLANTING.

A large number of garden crops, including melons, cucumbers, and beans, do not transplant readily from the seed bed to the open ground, and some special means for handling the plants must be employed where extra early planting is desired. A common practice among gardeners is to fill pint or quart berry boxes with good soil and plant a single hill in each box, as shown in figure 13.

Another method is to cut sods into pieces about 2 inches thick and 6 inches square and place them, root side upward, on the greenhouse bench or in the hotbed, the hills being planted in the loamy soil held in place by the roots of the grass. When the weather becomes sufficiently warm, and it is desired to set the plants in the garden, the berry boxes or pieces of sod are placed on a flat tray and carried to the place where the planting is to be done. Holes of sufficient size and depth are dug and the boxes or sods are simply buried at the points where it is desired to have the hills of plants. The boxes should be placed a little below the surface and fine earth worked in around the plants. If it is thought desirable, the bottoms of the boxes may be cut away when set in the garden.

FIG. 13.—Berry box used for starting and transplanting early plants.

### SETTING IN THE OPEN GROUND.

A few hours before removing plants from the seed bed or plant bed they should be well watered and the water allowed to soak into the soil. This will insure a portion of the soil adhering to the roots and prevent the plants from wilting. If the plants have been properly thinned or transplanted it is often possible to run a knife or trowel between them, thus cutting the soil into cubes that are transferred with them to the garden.

Where the soil does not adhere to the roots of the plants it is well to puddle them. In the process of puddling, a hole is dug in the earth near the plant bed, or a large pail may be used for the purpose, and a thin slime, consisting of clay, cow manure, and water, is prepared. The plants are taken in small bunches and their roots thoroughly coated with this mixture by dipping them up and down in the puddle a few times. Puddling insures a coating of moist earth over the entire root system of the plant, prevents the air from reaching the rootlets while on the way to the garden, and aids in securing direct contact between the roots and the soil.

Previous to setting out plants, the land should be worked over and put in good condition, and everything should be ready for quick operations when a suitable time arrives. The rows should be measured off, but it is well to defer making the furrows or digging the holes until ready to plant, in order to have the soil fresh. The time best suited for transferring plants from the plant bed to the open ground is when there is considerable moisture in the air and clouds obscure the sun, and if the plants can be set before a shower there will be no difficulty in getting them to grow. During seasons when there is very little rain at planting time, or in irrigated regions, evening is the best time to set the plants.

It is possible to set plants in quite dry soil, provided the roots are puddled and the earth well packed about them. When water is used in setting plants it should be applied after the hole has been partially filled, and the moist earth should then be covered with dry soil to prevent baking. Where water is available for irrigation it will be sufficient to puddle the roots and then irrigate after the plants are all in place.

FIG. 14.—Cross section of land illustrating the use of the dibble in setting plants. Improperly set plant on left.

Plants should be set a trifle deeper in the garden than they were in the plant bed. The majority of plants require to be set upright, and where the dibble is used for planting care should be taken that the soil is well pressed around the roots and no air spaces left. (Fig. 14.)

## TIME OF PLANTING.

No definite rule can be given regarding the time for planting seeds and plants in the garden, for the date varies with the locality and the time that it is desired to have the crop mature. A little practice will soon determine when and how often sowings should be made in order to escape frost and mature the crop at a time when it will be most useful. Certain crops will not thrive during the heated part of the summer, and their time of planting must be planned accordingly.

## PROTECTION OF PLANTS.

Some plants require protection from the direct rays of the sun in summer or from cold in winter, and there are many that need special protection while they are quite small. Seedlings of many of the garden crops are unable to force their way through the crust formed on the soil after heavy rains, and it is necessary either to break the crust with a steel rake or soften it by watering.

### PROTECTION FROM HEAT.

In parts of the country where the sunshine is extremely hot during a part of the summer, some plants, especially those that are grown for salad purposes, are benefited by shading. Shading is often used in the care of small plants when they are first transplanted.

Where boards are available they can be used for protecting plants that have been set in rows in the garden by placing them on the south side of the row at an angle that will cast a shadow over the plants, and holding them in place by short stakes driven in the ground, as shown in figure 15. Laths, wooden slats, cotton cloth, or shaded sash are frequently used to protect plant beds from the heat of summer.

FIG. 15.—Board used for protection of plants.

### PROTECTION FROM COLD.

For protecting plants from cold in winter several kinds of materials are used, such as boards, cloth, pine boughs, straw, manure, or leaves. There are a number of crops of a tropical nature that may be grown far north, provided they are properly protected during the winter.

Several of the annual crops can be matured much earlier in the spring if they are planted in the autumn and protected during the winter. Plants of this kind can often be protected by means of boards set at an angle on the north side of the row instead of on the south, as shown in figure 15. A mulch of manure, straw, or leaves forms a good protection, but care should be taken that the mulch does not contain seeds of any kind or serious trouble will attend the further cultivation of the crop. Plants are like animals in that they require air, and care should be exercised in putting on the winter covering not to smother them. Coarse, loose materials are better for a winter covering than fine, easily compacted substances.

## CULTIVATION OF GARDEN CROPS.

Frequent shallow cultivation should be employed for most garden crops, and during dry weather the depth should not exceed 2 inches. By keeping the surface soil well stirred what is termed a "dust mulch" is formed, and while this layer of finely divided soil will become quite dry it prevents the escape of moisture through the pores of the soil. A mulch consisting of fine manure, clippings from the lawn, or any similar material, spread to a distance of 10 or 12 inches around the plants will preserve the moisture; but the mulch should not be so heavy as to exclude the air.

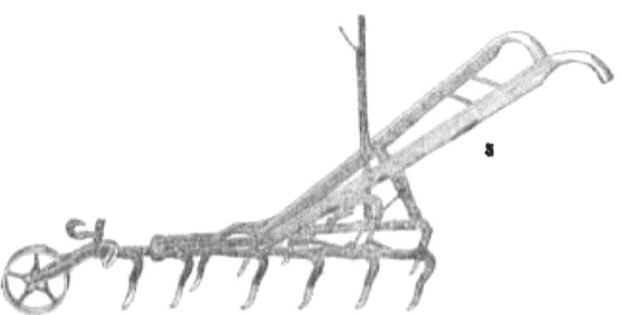

FIG. 16.—Small-tooth horse cultivator.

A crust forming over the soil after a rain or watering is detrimental to plant growth and should be broken up as soon as the land can be worked. To determine when the soil is sufficiently dry for cultivation, apply the usual test of squeezing in the hand. Sandy soils can be worked much sooner than clay soils after a rain. Too much importance can not be placed upon the matter of thorough cultivation of the garden, and if the work is promptly and properly done there will be little difficulty in controlling weeds.

### TOOLS FOR USE IN THE GARDEN.

There are a number of one-horse cultivators that are especially adapted for work in the garden. These may be provided with several sizes of teeth and shovels, and are easily transformed for various kinds of work (fig. 16). In working the crops while they

FIG. 17.—Spading fork.

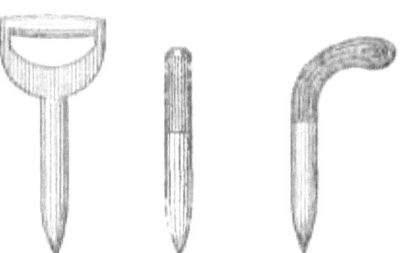

FIG. 18.—Dibbles used for transplanting.

are small the harrow or smaller teeth may be used, and later when the plants become larger the size of the shovels may be increased. Many gardeners, however, prefer to use the harrow teeth at all times.

When it is desirable to ridge up the soil around a crop, the wings, or hillers, may be put on either side of the cultivator. A one-horse turning plow is useful for running off rows or throwing up ridges similar to those shown in figure 4, page 10. Aside from the horse

FIG. 10.—Transplanting trowel.

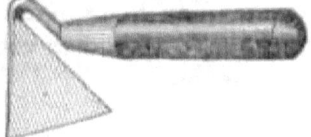
FIG. 20.—Onion hoe.

FIG. 21.—Hand weeder.

FIG. 22.—Thinning or weeding hook.

tools in general use on the farm, there are only one or two cultivators that will be required for the garden, and these are not expensive.

The outfit of hand tools for the garden should include a spade, a spading fork (fig. 17), a cut-steel rake, a 10-foot measuring pole, a line for laying off rows, a standard hoe, a narrow hoe, dibbles (fig. 18), a trowel (fig. 19), an assortment of hand weeders (figs. 20 to 22), a watering can, a wheelbarrow, and if the work is to be

FIG. 23.—Wheel hoe.

done largely by hand the outfit should also include some form of wheel hoe, of which there are a number on the market (fig. 23).

## IRRIGATION OF GARDEN CROPS.

Throughout the portions of the country where rains occur during the growing season it should not be necessary to irrigate in order to produce the ordinary garden crops. In arid regions, where irrigation must be depended upon for the production of crops, the system best adapted for use in that particular locality should be employed in the garden. Wherever irrigation is practiced the water should not be applied until needed, and then the soil should be thoroughly soaked.

After irrigation, the land should be cultivated as soon as the surface becomes sufficiently dry, and no more water should be applied until the plants begin to show the need of additional moisture. Constant or excessive watering is very detrimental in every case. Apply the water at any time of the day that is most convenient and when the plants require it.

By the subirrigation method of watering, lines of farm drain tiles or perforated pipes are laid on a level a few inches below the surface of the soil. This system is especially adapted for use in back-yard gardens where city water is available and where the area under cultivation is small. Subirrigation is expensive to install, as the lines of tiles should be about 3 feet apart, or one line for each standard row.

FIG. 24.—Cross section of soil showing arrangement of tiles for subirrigation.

By connecting the tiles at one end by means of a tile across the rows the water may be discharged into the tiles at one point from a hose, and will find its way to all parts of the system, entering the soil through the openings. A cross section of soil showing the proper arrangement of tiles is shown in figure 24.

For further information on irrigation see Farmers' Bulletin No. 138, entitled "Irrigation in Field and Garden."

## PRECAUTIONS TO AVOID ATTACKS OF INSECTS AND DISEASES.

In the control of insects and diseases that infest garden crops it is often possible to accomplish a great amount of good by careful sanitary management. In the autumn, after the crops have been harvested, or as fast as any crop is disposed of, any refuse that remains should be gathered and placed in the compost heap, or burned if diseased or infested with insects. Several of the garden insects find protection during the winter under boards and any loose material that may remain in the garden. Dead vines or leaves of plants are frequently covered with spores of diseases that affect those crops during the growing season, and these should be burned, as they possess very little fertilizing value.

For information on garden insects and their control address the Bureau of Entomology of this Department.

The diseases of garden crops are too numerous for attention in a publication of this nature. Specific information can be secured by addressing the Chief of the Bureau of Plant Industry of this Department.

# CULTURAL HINTS FOR GARDEN CROPS.

## ARTICHOKE, GLOBE.

Deep, rich sandy loam, with a liberal supply of well-rotted manure, is best suited for growing artichokes. Plant the seeds as soon as the soil is warm in the spring, and when the plants have formed three or four leaves they may be transplanted to rows 3 feet apart and 2 feet apart in the row. The plants do not produce until the second season, and in cold localities some form of covering will be necessary during the winter. This crop is not suited for cultivation north of the line of zero temperature.

Fig. 25.—Globe or bur artichoke.

After the bed is once established the plants may be reset each year by using the side shoots from the base of the old plants. If not reset the bed will continue to produce for several years, but the burs will not be so large as from new plants. The bur, or flower bud, as shown in figure 25, is the part used, and the burs should be gathered before the blossom part appears. If they are removed and no seed is allowed to form, the plants will continue to produce until the end of the season.

The heads, or burs, of the French artichoke are prepared for the table by boiling, and served with melted butter or with cream dressing.

## ARTICHOKE, JERUSALEM.

The Jerusalem artichoke will grow in any good garden soil, and should be planted 3 to 4 feet apart each way, with three or four small tubers in a hill. If large tubers are used for planting they should be cut the same as Irish potatoes. Plant as soon as the ground becomes warm in the spring and cultivate as for corn. A pint of tubers cut to eyes will plant about thirty hills. The tubers will be ready for use in October, but may remain in the ground and be dug at any time during the winter.

The tubers are prepared by boiling until soft, and are served with butter or creamed. They are also used for salads and pickles.

The Jerusalem artichoke is not of great importance as a garden vegetable, and the plant has a tendency to become a weed.

## ASPARAGUS.

Asparagus should have a place in every home vegetable garden where it will thrive. This crop can be grown on almost any well-drained soil, but will do best on a deep, mellow, sandy loam. There is little possibility of having the land too rich, and liberal applications of partly rotted barnyard manure should be made before the plants are set. The seeds of asparagus may be sown during the early spring in the rows where the plants are to remain and the seedlings thinned to stand 14 inches apart in the row at the end of the first season. It is usually more satisfactory to purchase two-year-old roots from some seedsman or dealer. (Fig. 26.) The price of good roots is generally about $1.25 per hundred, and one to two hundred plants will be found sufficient to supply the ordinary family. The roots should be transplanted during the late autumn or early spring.

Before setting out the plants the land should be loosened very deeply, either by subsoil plowing or deep spading. It is a good plan to remove the topsoil and spade manure into the subsoil to a depth of 14 or 16 inches; then replace the topsoil and add more manure. There are two methods of setting an asparagus bed, depending entirely upon the kind of cultivation to be employed in the garden. If horse tools are to be used, the plants should be set in rows 3½ feet apart and 14 inches apart in the row. On the other hand, if the garden space is limited the plants should be set in a solid bed, 1 foot apart each way, and cultivated by hand. In setting asparagus the crowns should be covered to a depth of 4 or 5 inches. At the North it will be desirable to mulch the asparagus bed during the winter with 3 or 4 inches of loose manure or straw. In the South the covering during the winter will not be necessary, but the bed should receive a dressing of manure or fertilizer at some time each year, preferably in the autumn.

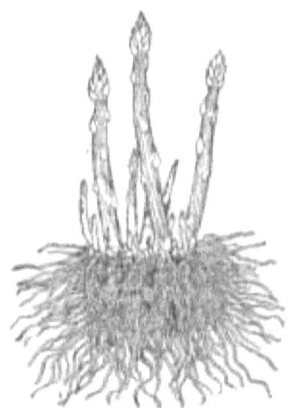

FIG. 26.—Asparagus plant.

The part of the asparagus used as a vegetable is the young shoots that are thrown up during the early spring. The shoots are removed when about 4 or 5 inches in length by cutting slightly below the surface of the ground, but care should be taken that the knife is not thrust at an angle or the crowns will be injured. If so desired, the shoots may be blanched by ridging up over the rows with loose, sandy soil or by allowing the mulch to remain and the shoots to make their way through it, but unblanched asparagus always has a better flavor than blanched, is more easily produced, and is most satisfactory for home use. Too heavy mulching has a tendency to retard the growth of the shoots by keeping the ground cold until late in the spring.

No shoots should be removed the first year the plants are set in the permanent bed, and the period of cutting should be short the second year. After the second year the plants become well established, and with proper fertilizing and care the bed will last indefinitely. During the cutting season all of the shoots should be removed, as the roots will cease to throw up shoots as soon as one is allowed to mature. When the shoots become tough and stringy, or are no longer desired for use, the cutting should cease and the tops should be allowed to grow during the summer. Late in the autumn, when the tops become dead, they can be removed and burned, the soil between the rows cultivated, and a fertilizer or mulch applied. For full information, see Farmers' Bulletin No. 61, entitled "Asparagus Culture."

There are several methods of preparing asparagus shoots for the table, the more common of which are as follows:

(1) Boil the shoots until tender in water to which a small quantity of salt has been added; serve while hot, as greens, with a little butter, vinegar, salt, and pepper.

(2) Boil as above and serve either with plain butter or creamed. The shoots can be cooked entire or cut into short pieces, and when creamed they are frequently served on toast.

## BEANS.

Beans thrive best in a rather warm sandy loam, but may be grown on almost any kind of soil. For the best results the soil should not be too rich in nitrogenous matter, or the plants will run to foliage and stems at the expense of the crop of pods. Heavy clay soils are not well adapted to bean culture, owing to the tendency of the soil to bake and prevent the seedlings from coming up evenly. The bean does not draw heavily upon the soil and is suitable for rotation with other garden crops.

Beans will not withstand frost, and the first plantings in the spring are frequently lost in this manner. It is very little trouble, however, to make a planting of beans, and the first planting should be made as soon as the ground is reasonably warm; this to be followed by a second and a third planting at intervals of about a week or ten days. It sometimes happens that the first planting will be killed by frost, and that the second will come through the ground immediately after the frost and mature several days ahead of those planted to replace the ones that were killed.

There are several classes of edible beans, including both climbing and bush sorts, all of which are valuable as foods and of great commercial importance. The various types and varieties of beans are too numerous for discussion here, and a few cultural hints only will be given.

In the cultivation of beans, the general rules for the care of garden crops should be adhered to, and frequent shallow stirring of the soil practiced. For a constant supply of bunch or snap beans successive plantings should be made, the final planting being made about eight weeks before time for frost in the autumn. In the South, plantings should be made as soon as the ground begins to warm, and continue until hot weather sets in. Toward the end of summer one or two plantings should be made for a fall crop.

For the production of bunch dry beans, such as Red Kidney, White Kidney, or White Marrow, plantings may be made almost any time during the first half of the summer. This class of bean is generally planted as late as possible to have the crop ripen just before early frost in the autumn. Bunch beans are generally planted in rows 30 inches apart, and the plants allowed to stand singly 3 or 4 inches apart, or they are planted in hills of 3 to 5 plants each, 12 to 15 inches apart. Good results may be obtained from planting Kidney or Marrow beans in the cornfield alongside the hills after the corn has been cultivated once or twice.

Pole beans require a somewhat richer soil than the bunch type, and should be planted in hills 3 by 4 or 4 by 4 feet, and, as the name implies, they require a pole or some similar support. Plant the seed during the early summer. Several varieties of climbing bean may be planted in the cornfield and allowed to climb upon the hills of corn. The old-fashioned corn bean belongs to this type.

The Lima bean, both pole and bush, forms one of the most desirable products of the garden. This crop thrives best when the soil is quite rich; in fact, good Lima beans can not be grown in poor soil. They should not be planted until the soil becomes thoroughly warm. Place the seed in hills, 8 or 10 to the hill, and after the plants become established thin to 4 or 5. The hills should be 4 or 5 feet apart for the pole varieties and 2 or 3 feet apart for the dwarf or bunch varieties. It is a good plan to make up the hill with a little additional manure well mixed with the soil. Cover the beans about 1½ inches, placing them with the eye downward.

When planting beans of any kind, the seed should not be covered to a greater depth than 2 inches when the soil is moderately dry, and if the soil is wet, the covering should be very slight.

For additional information the reader is referred to Farmers' Bulletin No. 121, entitled "Beans, Peas, and Other Legumes as Food."

## BEETS.

The red garden beet may be grown in any good soil, but rich sandy loam will give the best results. Sow the seeds in the spring as soon as danger of frost has passed. Beets should be planted in drills 12 to 18 inches apart, and when the plants are well up they should be thinned to 4 or 5 inches in the row. If desirable to plant in rows 3 feet apart for horse cultivation, the seeds may be sown in a double drill with 6 inches between, leaving 30 inches for cultivation. Two ounces of beet seed are required to plant 100 feet of row, or 5 pounds to the acre. As a rule each seed ball contains more than one seed, and this accounts for beets coming up very thickly. The seed should be covered to a depth of about 1 inch. For a succession of young beets during the summer, plantings should be made every four or five weeks during the spring months. Beets intended for winter storage should not be sown until late in the summer, the crop being harvested and stored in the same manner as turnips. Sugar beets are often substituted for the ordinary garden beet, especially for winter use.

Beets are used for pickles, or boiled, sliced, and fried in butter, adding a little vinegar just before removing from the fire. The young plants are used for greens.

## BORECOLE. (See KALE.)

## BRUSSELS SPROUTS.

This crop is closely related to cabbage and cauliflower, and may be grown in the same manner. Instead of a single head, Brussels sprouts form a large number of small heads in the axils of the leaves.

As the heads begin to crowd, the leaves should be broken from the stem of the plant to give them more room. A few leaves should be left at the top of the stem where the new heads are being formed. Brussels sprouts are more hardy than cabbage, and in mild climates may remain in the open ground all winter, the heads being removed as desired. For winter use in cold localities, take up plants that are well laden with heads and set them close together in a pit, cold frame, or cellar, with a little soil around the roots. The uses of Brussels sprouts are similar to those of cabbage, but they are considered to be of a superior flavor.

**BUR ARTICHOKE. (See ARTICHOKE, GLOBE.)**

**CABBAGE.**

For early spring cabbage in the South, sow the seeds in an outdoor bed and transplant to the garden before January 1. In the North, plant the seeds in a hotbed during February and set the plants in the open ground as early as the soil can be worked. For a late crop in the North, plant the seeds in a bed in the open ground in May or June and transplant to the garden in July. Early cabbages require a rich, warm soil in order that they may mature early. For late cabbages the soil should be heavier and more retentive of moisture and not so rich as for the early crop, as the heads are liable to burst. Cabbages should be set in rows 30 to 36 inches apart and 14 to 18 inches apart in the row. Where the plants are set out in the autumn and allowed to remain in the ground over winter, they are usually placed on top of ridges, as shown in figure 4, page 10. Early cabbage must be used soon after it has formed solid heads, as it will not keep during hot weather.

Late cabbage may be buried in pits or stored in cellars or specially constructed houses. The usual method of storing cabbage is to dig a trench about 18 inches deep and 3 feet wide and set the cabbage upright, with the heads close together and the roots bedded in soil. As cold weather comes on, the heads are covered slightly with straw and then 3 or 4 inches of earth put on. Slight freezing does not injure cabbage, but it should not be subjected to repeated freezing and thawing. If stored in a cellar or building, the heads are generally cut from the stems and stored on slatted shelves or in shallow bins. While in storage, cabbage should be well ventilated and kept as cool as possible without freezing.

**CANTALOUPE. (See MELON—MUSKMELON.)**

**CARDOON.**

The cardoon is a thistle-like plant, very similar in appearance to the Globe artichoke, but is grown as an annual. The seeds are sown in early spring in a hotbed or cold frame and the plants transplanted later to the open ground. The cardoon should be planted in rows 3 feet apart and 18 inches apart in the row on rich soil, where it can secure plenty of moisture and make rapid growth. Toward autumn the leaves are drawn together and the center blanched in the same manner as endive. If intended for winter use, the leaves are not blanched in the garden, but the plants are lifted with considerable earth adhering to the roots and stored closely in a dark pit or cellar to blanch.

The blanched leaf stems are used for making salads, soups, and stews.

## CARROT.

The culture of the carrot is practically the same as the parsnip, except that carrots are not thinned so much and are allowed to grow almost as thickly as planted. Carrots should be dug in the autumn and stored the same as parsnips or turnips. Any surplus can be fed sparingly to horses, mules, or cattle.

The roots of the carrot are used at all times of the year, mostly in soups, but they may be boiled and served with butter or creamed.

## CAULIFLOWER.

Cauliflower requires a rich, moist soil, and thrives best under irrigation. Cauliflower will not withstand as much frost as cabbage. The culture is the same as for cabbage until the heads begin to develop, after which the leaves may be tied together over the heads in order to exclude the light and keep the heads white.

The tender heads of cauliflower are boiled and served with butter, or creamed, and are also used for pickling.

## CELERIAC.

A large-rooted form of celery used for cooking only. Cultivate the same as celery, but banking or blanching is not required. The roots may remain in the ground until wanted for use, provided a light covering be applied to prevent freezing.

## CELERY.

For the North sow the seed in a hotbed or cold frame and transplant to the open ground. Celery plants are generally improved by transplanting twice. In the South the plants are not started until late in the summer and the crop is matured during the early winter. Celery seeds are very small and are slow in germinating, and the temperature of the seed bed should be kept low. The seed bed should be especially well prepared and the seeds should not be covered to a greater depth than one-eighth of an inch. Watering should be attended to very carefully and the bed should not dry out. After the plants are up care should be taken that the bed does not become too wet and the plants damp off. Five hundred plants will be sufficient for the ordinary family, and they should be set 6 inches apart in rows 3 to 5 feet apart.

Celery requires a deep, rich, moist soil, with plenty of well-rotted barnyard manure or fertilizer and frequent shallow cultivation. In the garden celery may be planted after some early crop, such as lettuce, radishes, peas, or beans. As soon as the plants attain considerable size the leaves should be drawn up and a little soil compacted about the base of the plant to hold it upright. If the blanching is done with earth, care should be taken that the hearts of the plants do not become filled. Boards, paper, drain tiles, or anything that will exclude the light may be used for blanching, but earthing up will produce the finest flavor.

Celery may be kept for winter use by banking with earth and covering the tops by means of leaves or straw to keep it from freezing, or it may be dug and removed to a cellar, cold frame, vacant hotbed, or pit, and reset close together, with the roots bedded in earth. While in storage celery should be kept as cool as possible without freezing.

The blanched stems of celery are eaten in the raw state, and both the stems and enlarged roots are stewed and creamed. Celery seed is used for flavoring soups and pickles.

For further information on celery read Farmers' Bulletin No. 148, entitled "Celery Culture."

### CHERVIL.

Under the name of chervil two distinct plants, known as salad chervil and the turnip-rooted chervil, are cultivated. The seeds of the salad chervil are sown in spring and the crop will thrive on any good garden soil. The seeds of the turnip-rooted chervil should be sown in the early autumn, but they will not germinate until the following spring.

The edible part of this plant is the root, which somewhat resembles the carrot and is used in the same manner. The leaves are used the same as parsley for garnishing and in flavoring soups.

### CHICORY.

Chicory is grown for two or three purposes. The root of this plant is the common adulterant of coffee, and large quantities are used for this purpose. The commercial growing of chicory is confined to a few sections, as the crop will not thrive on every kind of soil.

A deep, rich loam, without excessive amounts of clay or sand, is desirable, and soil that is not too rich in nitrogenous matter is best suited to the production of roots.

The roots of chicory are frequently placed in soil under a greenhouse bench or in a warm cellar and covered with a foot or more of straw, or with a light covering of straw and then several inches of warm manure. Under this covering the leaves will be formed in a solid head, which is known on the market as witloof.

Chicory has run wild in some parts of the country and is considered a bad weed. The handsome blue flowers of the chicory, which are borne the second season, are very attractive.

As a pot herb chicory is used like spinach, but the leaves should be boiled in two waters to remove the bitter taste. As a salad the roots are dug in the autumn and planted in cellars or under a greenhouse bench, where they produce an abundance of blanched leaves, which are eaten raw. The blanched leaves are also boiled and used as greens.

### CHIVE.

This is a small onion-like plant having flat, hollow leaves which are used for flavoring soups. The chive rarely forms seeds, and it is propagated by the bulbs, which grow in clusters. (Fig. 27.) The leaves may be cut freely and are soon replaced by others.

### CIBOL. (See ONION.)

### CITRON.

The citron is a type of watermelon with solid flesh which is used for preserves and sweetpickles. The rind of the watermelon is frequently substituted for citron. The cultivation of the citron is the same as for the watermelon.

### CIVE. (See CHIVE.)

### COLLARDS.

The culture and uses of collards are the same as for cabbage and kale. Collards withstand the heat better than either cabbage or kale, and a type known as Georgia collards is highly esteemed in the Southern States. Collards do not form a true head, but instead a loose rosette of leaves, which, when blanched, are very tender and of delicate flavor.

### CORN SALAD.

Corn salad is also known as lamb's-lettuce and fetticus. Sow the seed during the early spring in drills 14 to 18 inches apart and cultivate the same as for lettuce or mustard. For an extra early crop the seed may be planted during the autumn and the plants covered lightly during the winter. In the Southern States the covering will not be necessary and the plants will be ready for use during February and March. The leaves are frequently used in their natural green state, but they may be blanched by covering the rows with anything that will exclude the light. Corn salad is used as a salad in place of lettuce, or mixed with lettuce or water cress. The flavor of corn salad is very mild, and it is improved by mixing with some other salad plant for use. It is also boiled with mustard for greens.

FIG. 27.—Chive.

### CORN, SWEET.

Plant sweet corn as soon as the soil is warm in the spring, and make successive plantings every two weeks until July, or the same result can be attained to some extent by a careful selection of early, medium, and late varieties. Plant the seeds in drills 3 feet apart and thin to a single stalk every 10 to 14 inches, or plant 5 to 6 seeds in hills 3 feet apart each way, and thin out to 3 to 5 stalks in a hill. Cover the seeds about 2 inches deep. Cultivate frequently and keep down all weeds, removing suckers from around the base of the stalk.

Sweet corn should be planted on rich land, and the method of cultivation is practically the same as for field corn, but should be more thorough. There are a number of good early varieties, and for a midsummer and late sort there is none better than Stowell's Evergreen.

## CRESS.

Under the name of cress there are two forms, the water cress and the upland cress. The upland cress, sometimes called peppergrass, is easily grown from seed sown in drills a foot apart. As the plants last but a short time, it will be necessary to make a sowing every few days if a continuous supply is desired.

Water cress can be grown all the year in small open ditches containing running spring water. It is best and most easily produced in water from rather warm springs in limestone regions. A sufficient supply for family use can be grown in a small spring-fed brook, and the plants may be started either from small pieces of plants or from seed. Cress is used in salads, to which it imparts a pleasant pungency.

## CUCUMBER.

The soil for cucumbers should be a rich sandy loam, rather moist, but not wet. Plant in hills 4 feet apart each way as soon as all danger of frost is past. It is a good plan to work thoroughly a shovelful of well-rotted manure or a small handful of fertilizer into each hill in addition to the regular manuring of the land. The manure in the hill will give the plants a good start. Cucumbers are frequently planted in drills about 7 feet apart and thinned to 12 or 18 inches apart in the row. If it is desirable to secure extra early cucumbers, the plants may be started in a hotbed and transplanted to the garden by means of berry boxes. (Fig. 13.) At the South, cucumbers are planted in the open ground as early as February or March. Cucumber seedlings are easily injured by cold, even where no frost occurs, and throughout the northern part of the country the planting should be deferred until the soil is warm.

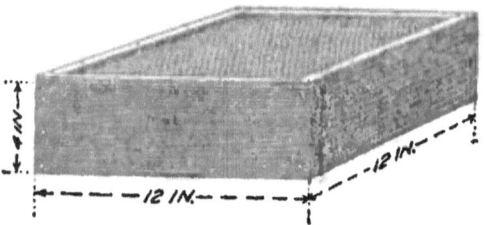

FIG. 28.—Device for protecting young cucumber plants.

While young the cucumber plants are frequently destroyed by a small beetle that attacks the lower part of the stem and the under side of the leaves. To preserve the plants some remedy will be necessary, and, where only a few hills are grown for family use the beetles may be kept off by covering the plants with frames over which fly screen or mosquito netting has been stretched, as shown in figure 28. Another method of protecting the plants is to set an arch of wire or one-half of a barrel hoop over the hill and spread a piece of mosquito netting over this support. The edges of the netting may be held down by covering with earth, and as soon as the plants are beyond danger of attack the netting may be stored for future use.

For further information on the protection of cucumber plants from the striped beetle see Circulars 31 and 59 of the Bureau of Entomology.

Cucumbers should receive frequent shallow cultivation until the vines begin to run freely; after this very little attention is required except to pull out stray weeds as they may appear. In order to keep the vines in good bearing condition, no fruit should be allowed to ripen, and when grown for pickles the fruits should all be removed while quite small.

As cucumbers are subject to several diseases, the old vines and fruits should all be destroyed and the crop should not be planted two years in succession on the same land. As a rule garden cucumbers and melons will not be greatly injured by diseases. Full information on this subject can be secured by consulting Farmers' Bulletin No. 231, entitled "Spraying for Cucumber and Melon Diseases."

### DANDELION.

Sow the seed of dandelion in spring in drills 18 inches apart, covering it one-half inch deep. Thin the plants to about 12 inches apart and give good clean cultivation throughout the summer. In the colder parts of the country it may be desirable to mulch slightly during the winter to prevent the plants heaving out of the soil. Early the following spring the plants will be ready for use as greens, but they are greatly improved if blanched by setting two boards in the form of an inverted letter V over the row. The blanching not only makes the leaves more tender but destroys a part of the bitter taste. Dandelion greens should be boiled in two waters to remove the bitterness.

### EGGPLANT.

The plants for this crop should be started and handled in the same manner as described for the tomato. After the weather has become settled and the ground quite warm, set the plants in the garden in rows 3 feet apart and 2 feet apart in the row. The soil best adapted to the production of eggplant is a fine, rich sandy loam and should be well drained. Cultivate freely and keep the plants growing rapidly. Many growers believe that fresh stable manure should not be used in connection with the growing of eggplant and that the land should not contain unfermented vegetable matter to any extent.

Eggplant is used in several ways, among which are the following: Peel and cut into slices one-half inch thick, soak in salt water one hour; boil until tender; then coat with rolled crackers or flour and fry in butter or fat. Another method is to steam or bake the eggplant whole and serve in the shell, the pulp being eaten with salt, pepper, and butter.

### ENDIVE.

The endive is a form of chicory. Sow the seeds thinly in drills, and when the plants are well established thin to 8 inches. Water and cultivate thoroughly in order that a good growth of leaves may be made. When the leaves are 6 to 8 inches in length draw them together and tie them so the heart will blanch. The leaves should not be tied up while wet or decay will follow. The heads should be used as soon as blanched. For winter use sow the seeds rather late and remove the plants, with a ball of earth adhering to the roots, to a cellar or cold frame, and blanch during the winter as required for use.

Endive is used as a salad at times of the year when lettuce and similar crops are out of season.

### FETTICUS. (See CORN SALAD.)

### FLAG. (See LEEK.)

**FRENCH ARTICHOKE. (See ARTICHOKE, GLOBE.)**

**GARLIC.**

Garlic is closely allied to the onion, but will remain in the ground from one year to another if undisturbed. Garlic is planted by setting the small bulbs, or cloves, either in the autumn or early spring. The culture is practically the same as for the onion. The bulbs are used for flavoring purposes.

**GEORGIA COLLARDS. (See COLLARDS.)**
**GERMAN CELERY. (See CELERIAC.)**
**GROUND CHERRY. (See PHYSALIS.)**
**GUMBO. (See OKRA.)**
**HORSE-RADISH.**

Horse-radish will thrive best in a deep, rich soil, where there is plenty of moisture. The rows should be 3 feet apart and the plants 12 to 18 inches apart in the row. Tops cut from large roots or pieces of small roots are used for planting. A comparatively few hills of horse-radish will be sufficient for family use, and the roots required for starting can be secured of seedsmen for 25 or 30 cents a dozen. This crop will require no particular cultivation except to keep down the weeds, and is inclined to become a weed itself if not controlled.

The large fleshy roots are prepared for use by peeling and grating. The grated root is treated with a little salt and vinegar and served as a relish with meats, oysters, etc. The roots should be dug during the winter or early spring before the leaves start. After being treated with salt and vinegar the grated root may be bottled for summer use.

**HUSK TOMATO. (See PHYSALIS.)**
**IRISH POTATO. (See POTATO, IRISH.)**
**JERUSALEM ARTICHOKE. (See ARTICHOKE, JERUSALEM.)**
**KALE, OR BORECOLE.**

There are a large number of forms of kale, and these are thought by some to be the original type of the cabbage. Kale does not form a head and has convoluted leaves and thick leaf stems. It is cultivated the same as cabbage, but may be set somewhat closer. This crop is very hardy and will live through the winter in the open ground in localities where freezing is not too severe. The flavor of kale is improved by frost.

Kale is used for greens during the winter, and as a substitute for cabbage.

**KOHL-RABI.**

Kohl-rabi belongs to the same class as cabbage and cauliflower, but presents a marked variation from either. It is, perhaps, half-way between the cabbage and turnip, in that its edible part consists of the swollen stem of the plant, as shown in figure 29. For an early crop, plant and cultivate the same as for early cabbage. For a late crop or for all seasons in the South the seed may be sown in drills where the crop is to be grown and thinned

FIG. 29.—Kohl-rabi.

to about 8 inches apart in the row. The rows should be from 18 to 36 inches apart, according to the kind of cultivation employed. The fleshy stems should be used while they are young and quite tender.

Prepare kohl-rabi for the table in the same manner as turnips, which it very much resembles when cooked.

### LAMB'S-LETTUCE. (See CORN SALAD.)

### LEEK.

This plant belongs to the same class as does the onion, but requires somewhat different treatment. Leeks can be grown on any good garden soil and are usually sown in a shallow trench. The plants should be thinned to stand about 4 inches apart in the row and the cultivation should be similar to that for onions. After the plants have attained almost full size the earth is drawn around them to the height of 6 or 8 inches to blanch the fleshy stem. The leek does not form a true bulb like the onion, but the stem is uniformly thick throughout. Leeks are marketed in bunches like young onions, and they may be stored the same as celery for winter.

Leeks are used for flavoring purposes and are boiled and served with a cream dressing the same as young onions.

### LETTUCE.

This crop attains its best development in a rich sandy loam in which there is plenty of organic matter. Lettuce thrives best during the early spring or late autumn and will not withstand the heat of summer. In order that the leaves may be crisp and tender, it is necessary to force the growth. The usual method of growing lettuce for home use is to sow the seeds broadcast in a bed and remove the leaves from the plants as rapidly as they become large enough for use. A much better method is either to thin or transplant the seedlings and allow the plants to form rather compact heads and then cut the entire plant for use.

In the Southern States the seeds may be sown during the autumn and the plants allowed to remain in the ground over winter. At the North the seeds may be sown in a hotbed or cold frame and the seedlings transplanted to the open ground, or the seeding may be in rows in the garden and the plants thinned to 5 or 6 inches in the row. Lettuce may be grown in rows about 12 inches apart. In order to produce crisp and tender lettuce during the summer months, it may be necessary to provide some form of partial shading.

### MELON—MUSKMELON.

A sandy loam with plenty of well-rotted barnyard manure will be found to be adapted to the cultivation of the muskmelon. When commercial fertilizer is used instead of manure, it should be applied at the rate of from 500 to 1,000 pounds of high-grade material to the acre. The muskmelon requires a long season to develop and is easily injured by frost or even by cool weather.

For an early crop in the North, start the hills in a hotbed in berry boxes and plant out after the soil becomes warm. For the main crop throughout the country the seeds are planted in the open ground as soon as the soil is reasonably warm. Place the hills about 6 feet apart each way and 8 or 10 seeds in a hill. After the plants become established, thin out all but the four best ones. Another method is to sow in drills and thin to single plants 18 inches to 2 feet apart. Good cultivation should be maintained until the vines interfere.

Muskmelons are subject to a number of diseases, and while the plants are quite young they are attacked by the cucumber beetle. The same precautionary measures as are recommended in the case of cucumbers should be observed for both troubles.

There are a number of good varieties of muskmelons, and the Rocky Ford, or Netted Gem, is one of the best.

### MELON—WATERMELON.

The cultivation of the watermelon is practically the same as for the muskmelon, except that the plants grow larger and require more room for development than those of the muskmelon. Watermelons require that the soil should contain a larger percentage of sand than muskmelons, and that the land should be quite rich. Watermelons should be planted 10 feet each way between the hills, or in drills 10 feet apart and thinned to 3 feet apart in the drills. The watermelon seedlings must be protected from the cucumber beetle until the foliage becomes toughened.

### MULTIPLIER ONION. (See ONION.)

### MUSKMELON. (See MELON—MUSKMELON.)

### MUSTARD.

Almost any good soil will produce a crop of mustard. The basal leaves of mustard are used for greens, and as the plants require but a short time to reach the proper stage for use frequent sowings should be made. Sow the seeds thickly in drills as early as possible in the spring, or for late use sow the seeds in September or October. The forms of white mustard, of which the leaves are often curled and frilled, are generally used. Mustard greens are cooked like spinach.

### NEW ZEALAND SPINACH.

The plant known as New Zealand spinach is not a true spinach, but grows much larger and should be planted in rows 3 feet apart, with the plants 12 to 18 inches apart in the row. Some difficulty may be experienced in getting the seeds to germinate, and they should be soaked one or two hours in hot water before planting. New Zealand spinach is satisfactory for growing in warm climates, as it withstands heat better than the ordinary spinach. The fleshy leaves and tender stems are cooked the same as spinach.

### OKRA, OR GUMBO.

Sow the seeds of okra in the open after the ground has become quite warm, or start the plants in berry boxes in a hotbed and transplant them to the garden after all danger of frost is past. The rows should be 4 feet apart for the dwarf sorts and 5 feet apart for the tall kinds, with the plants 2 feet apart in the row. Okra does best in rather rich land and requires frequent shallow cultivation until the plants cover the ground.

The young pods are the part used, and these are employed principally in soups, to which they impart a pleasant flavor and mucilaginous consistency. If the pods are removed from the plants and none allowed to ripen, the plants will continue to produce pods until killed by frost, but the best pods are grown on young plants. Okra pods can be dried or canned for winter use.

For further information on okra, see Farmers' Bulletin No. 232, entitled "Okra: Its Culture and Uses."

### ONIONS.

A rich sandy loam containing plenty of humus is best suited to the production of onions. This crop has been grown very successfully on the muck beds of the States bordering on the Great Lakes. The usual plan on a small scale is to plant one or two quarts of "sets" in drills 12 to 18 inches apart and 2 to 3 inches apart in the row, covering about an inch deep. When a large acreage is to be grown the soil is made very fine and smooth and the onion seed is sown in drills and then thinned to 2 or 3 inches apart after the plants become established. For the best results from seed, sow in cold frames during the fall or in a hotbed in the early spring and transplant to the open ground as soon as the soil is in good condition to work. Figure 30 shows an ideal stand of onions.

FIG 30.—Onions.

FIG. 31.—Cross section of Potato or Multiplier onion.

Onions require frequent shallow cultivation and it may be necessary to resort to hand work in order to keep the crop free from weeds. If it is desired to hasten the maturity of the bulbs by preventing continued growth of the tops, this may be accomplished by rolling an empty barrel over the rows and breaking down the tops. After the tops are practically dead the onion bulbs should be removed from the soil and spread in a dry, well ventilated place to cure, after which they may be stored in crates or bags for winter use.

There are several kinds of onions that may remain in the soil over winter. The Multiplier or Potato onion can be planted from sets in the autumn and will produce excellent early green onions. This type of onion is peculiar in that a large onion contains a number of distinct hearts, as shown in

FIG. 32.—Top or Tree onion, producing bulblets on top of stem.

figure 31, and if planted will produce a number of small onions. On the other hand, a small onion contains but one heart and will produce a large onion. A few large onions should be planted each year to produce the sets for the following year's planting.

Another variety is the Top or Tree onion, which produces a large number of bulblets above ground on the top of a stem, as shown in figure 32. The small bulbs can be planted in the autumn and will produce onions the following season.

The small onion known as the shallot is frequently planted in early spring for its small bulbs, or "cloves," which are used in the same manner as onions. The leaves are also used for flavoring.

The cibol or Welsh onion is grown either from seeds or bulbs. Where the climate is not severe, the seed may be sown in the autumn, and the leaves, which are used for flavoring soups, will be ready for use in the spring.

For additional information on the onion, see Farmers' Bulletin No. 39, entitled "Onion Culture."

### OYSTER-PLANT. (See SALSIFY.)

### PARSLEY.

After soaking the seeds of parsley for a few hours in warm water, they may be sown in the same manner as celery seed and the plants transplanted to the open ground. At the North, parsley will live over winter in a cold frame or pit, and in the South it will thrive in the open ground during the winter, but it can not withstand the heat of summer. The plants should be set in rows 12 inches apart and every 4 inches in the row.

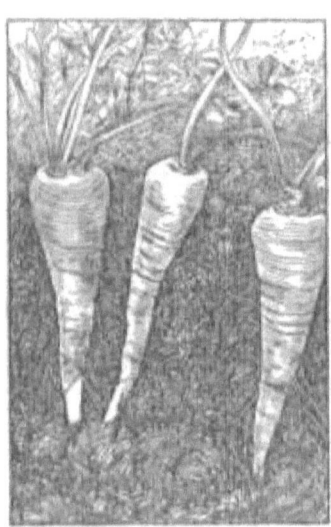

FIG. 33.—Parsnips.

The leaves of parsley are used for garnishings around meats and for flavoring soups.

### PARSNIP.

Sow the seeds of parsnip as early as convenient in the spring in drills 18 inches to 3 feet apart. Thin the plants to stand 3 inches apart in the rows. The parsnip requires a rich soil and frequent cultivation. The roots can be dug late in the fall and stored in cellars or pits, or allowed to remain where grown and dug as required for use. (Fig. 33.) It is considered best to allow the roots to become frozen in the ground, as the freezing improves their flavor. As soon as the roots begin to grow the following spring they will no longer be fit for use. All roots not used during the winter should be dug and removed from the garden, as they will produce seed the second season and become of a weedy nature. When the parsnip has been allowed to run wild the root is considered to be poisonous.

To prepare parsnip for the table, boil the roots until tender and then cut in slices and brown in butter. They may also be roasted with meat the same as potatoes.

## PEAS.

Garden peas require a rather rich and friable soil with good drainage in order that the first plantings may be made early in the spring. Fertilizers that are high in nitrogenous matter should not be applied to the land immediately before planting, as they will have a tendency to produce too great growth of vines at the expense of pods. Land that has been well manured the previous year will be found satisfactory without additional fertilizer. A sandy loam is to be preferred for growing peas, but a good crop may be produced on clay soils; however, the pods will be a few days later in forming. Peas are easily grown and form one of the most palatable of garden products.

The first plantings should be of such varieties as Alaska or Gradus, which make a small but quick growth, and may or may not be provided with supports. The dwarf sorts like American Wonder come on later, require very little care, and produce peas of fine quality. The tall-growing sorts of the Telephone type are desirable for still later use on account of their large production and excellent quality. Sugar peas have tender pods and if gathered very young the pods may be eaten in the same manner as snap beans. In order to maintain a continuous supply of fresh peas, plantings should be made every ten days or two weeks during the spring months, beginning as soon as the ground can be worked. In the extreme South peas may be grown during the entire winter.

For the best results peas should be planted in the bottom of a furrow 6 inches in depth and the seeds covered with not more than 2 or 3 inches of soil. If the soil is heavy the covering should be less than 2 inches. After the plants attain a height of 4 or 5 inches the soil should be worked in around them until the trench is filled. The rows for peas should be 3 feet apart for the dwarf sorts and 4 feet apart for the tall kinds. A pint of seed will plant about 100 feet of single row. Many growers follow the practice of planting in a double row with a 6-inch space between. The double-row method is especially adapted for the varieties that require some form of support, as a trellis can be placed between the two rows.

Brush stuck in the ground will answer for a support for the peas to climb upon. Three-foot poultry netting makes a desirable trellis. If peas are planted for autumn use, the earliest varieties should be employed.

## PEPPERS.

Plant the seed of peppers in a hotbed, and transplant to the open ground as soon as it is warm, or sow the seeds in the garden after all danger of frost is past. When grown in the garden the plants should be in rows 3 feet apart and 15 to 18 inches apart in the row. The plants require about the same treatment as the tomato. There are a large number of varieties of the pepper, including the large sweet sorts used for pickling and the small hot kinds, such as Chili, Tabasco, and Cayenne.

## PEPPERGRASS. (See CRESS.)

## PHYSALIS.

The physalis is also known as the ground-cherry or husk-tomato. Sow the seed in a hotbed or cold frame and transplant to the garden after danger of frost is past, or the seeds may be sown in the row where the plants are to remain and thinned to 12 or 18 inches. No particular care is required except to keep them free from weeds. There are a large number of varieties of the physalis, and the fruits vary in size and color. The variety commonly used in gardens produces a bright-yellow fruit, which is about the size of an ordinary cherry. Toward fall the fruits will drop to the ground and will be protected for some time by their husks. If gathered and placed in a cool place the fruits will keep for a long time. The physalis will self-sow and may become a weed, but it is easily controlled. A few of the volunteer plants may be lifted in the spring and placed in rows instead of making a special sowing of seed. Ten plants will produce all the husk-tomatoes desired by the average family. The fruits are excellent for making preserves and marmalade.

#### PIE-PLANT. (See RHUBARB.)

#### POTATO, IRISH.

A rich, sandy loam is best suited to the production of Irish potatoes, and the fertilizers employed should contain high percentages of potash. The main crop of Irish potatoes for family use should be grown elsewhere, but a small area of early ones properly belongs in the garden. The preparation of the soil should be the same as for general garden crops.

Early potatoes should be planted as early in the spring as it is feasible to work the land, irrespective of locality. This will require planting in January in the extreme Southern States, and as late as May in the extreme Northern States. Late potatoes are extensively grown in the North, and the planting should be done late in May or during June. The rows should be 2½ to 3 feet apart, and the hills 14 to 18 inches apart in the row. Lay off the rows with a one-horse plow or lister, and drop the seed, one or two pieces in a place, in the bottom of the furrow. Cover the seed to a depth of about 4 inches, using a hoe or a one-horse plow for the purpose. One to three weeks will be required for the potatoes to come up, depending entirely upon the temperature of the soil. The ground may freeze slightly after the planting has been done, but so long as the frost does not reach the seed potatoes no harm will result, and growth will begin as soon as the soil becomes sufficiently warm.

As soon as the potatoes appear above the ground and the rows can be followed, the surface soil should be well stirred by means of one of the harrow-toothed cultivators. Good cultivation should be maintained throughout the growing season, with occasional hand hoeing, if necessary, to keep the ground free from weeds. Toward the last the soil may be well worked up around the plants to hold them erect and protect the tubers from the sun after the vines begin to die.

After digging the potatoes they should not be allowed to lie exposed to the sun or to any light while in storage, as they soon become green and unfit for table use. Early potatoes especially should not be stored in a damp place during the heated part of the summer, and will keep best if covered with straw in a cool, shady shed until the autumn weather sets in, after which they can be placed in a dry cellar or buried in the open ground. The ideal temperature for keeping Irish potatoes is between 36° and 40° F., but they will not withstand any freezing.

## 41

**POTATO ONION.** (See ONION.)

**POTATO, SWEET.**

The sweet potato is of a tropical nature and succeeds best in the warm, sandy loam soils of the Southern States. Sweet potatoes are, however, grown commercially as far north as the southern line of the State of Pennsylvania, and for family use even in southern New York and Michigan. A warm, loose sandy soil is best adapted to the production of sweet potatoes, and good drainage is essential. In order to improve the drainage conditions, it is customary to set the plants on top of ridges which are thrown up by means of a plow, two furrows being turned together. For best results the soil should be well fertilized throughout, but in commercial sweet potato culture the plan is frequently adopted of placing the fertilizer or manure in a furrow and then turning the ridge up over it, as shown in figure 4. The manure should be evenly distributed, and it is advisable to run a cultivator once or twice in the furrow to mix the manure with the soil. Too much manure in one spot under the hill will produce a large growth of vine at the expense of the potatoes.

Toward the northern part of the area over which sweet potatoes are grown it is necessary to start the plants in a hotbed in order that the length of season may be sufficient to mature the crop. The roots that are too small for marketing are used for seed, and these are bedded close together in the hotbed and covered with about 2 inches of sand or fine soil, such as leaf mold. The seed should be bedded about five or six weeks before it will be safe to set the plants in the open ground, which is usually about May 15 or May 20. Toward the last the hotbed should be ventilated very freely in order to harden off the plants.

The ridges for planting sweet potatoes should be 3 to 5 feet apart and the plants about 14 inches apart in the row. Cultivate sufficiently to keep the surface soil loose and free from weeds, and the vines will soon cover the ground, after which no cultivation will be necessary. In the warmer parts of the country the seed is not bedded, but is cut in small pieces and planted in the ridges instead of plants. After the plants come up and begin to make vines freely, pieces of the vines are removed and used as cuttings for planting additional areas, the cuttings taking root and growing the same as plants grown from seed. In this manner 3 and 4 plantings are made, the last being as late as the middle of July. If a rainy spell be selected for making and planting the cuttings, very few will fail to grow, and an excellent crop may be produced.

To the north, sweet potatoes are dug as soon as the vines are nipped by frost. In the South the potatoes are allowed to remain in the ground until a convenient time for handling them, and in Florida or Texas they are frequently left until required for use. Sweet potatoes should be dug on a bright, drying day when the soil is not too wet. On a small scale they may be dug with a spading fork, and great care should be taken that the roots do not become bruised or injured in the process of handling. It is desirable that the roots should lie exposed for two or three hours to dry thoroughly, after which they may be placed in a warm, well ventilated room to cure for several days. The proper temperature for curing sweet potatoes is from 80° to 90° F. and 45° or 55° F. afterwards. A small crop may be cured around the kitchen stove, and later stored in a dry room where there will be no danger of their becoming too cold. Sweet potatoes should be handled as little as possible, especially after they have been cured.

Sweet potatoes are used the same as Irish potatoes, and may also be employed in making pies the same as squash. For further information the reader should obtain Farmers' Bulletin No. 129, entitled "Sweet Potatoes."

### PUMPKIN.

The true pumpkin is hardly to be considered as a garden crop, and, as a rule, should be planted among the field corn. Plant where the hills of corn are missing and cultivate with the corn.

### RADISH.

The radish is quite hardy and may be grown throughout the winter in hotbeds at the North, in cold frames in the latitude of Washington, and in the open ground in the South. For the home garden the seed should be sown in the open ground as soon as the soil is moderately warm. Plant in drills 12 to 18 inches apart, and as soon as the plants are up thin them slightly to prevent crowding. Radishes require to be grown on a quick, rich soil, and some of the earlier sorts can be matured in two to three weeks after planting. If the radishes grow slowly they will have a pungent flavor and will not be fit for table use. For a constant supply successive plantings should be made every two weeks, as the roots lose their crispness and delicate flavor if allowed to remain long in the open ground. As a rule a large percentage of radish seed will grow, and it is often possible by careful sowing to avoid the necessity of thinning, the first radishes being pulled as soon as they are of sufficient size for table use, thus making room for those that are a little later. Radishes will not endure hot weather and are suited to early spring and late autumn planting.

There are a number of varieties of winter radishes, the seed of which may be planted the latter part of summer and the roots pulled and stored for winter use. These roots should remain in the ground as long as possible without frosting and should then be dug and stored the same as turnips. This type of radish will not compare with the earlier summer varieties, which may be easily grown in a hotbed or cold frame during the winter. One ounce of radish seed is sufficient to plant 100 feet of row, and when grown on a large scale 10 to 12 pounds of seed will be required to the acre.

### RHUBARB.

The soil for rhubarb should be deep, and there is little danger of having it too rich. Like asparagus the seedling plants of rhubarb can be grown and transplanted. Ten to twelve good hills are sufficient to produce all the rhubarb required by the average family, and these are most easily established by planting pieces of roots taken from another bed. Good roots may be secured from dealers and seedsmen at about $1.50 a dozen. The old hills may be divided in the early spring or late fall by digging away the earth on one side and cutting the hill in two with a sharp spade, the part removed being used to establish a new hill.

The usual method of planting rhubarb is to set the plants in a single row along the garden fence, and the hills should be about 4 feet apart. If more than one row is planted the hills should be 3½ or 4 feet each way. The thick leaf stems are the part used, and none should be pulled from the plants the first year after setting. Rhubarb should receive the same treatment during winter as asparagus, and the plants should never be allowed to ripen seed. The roots may be brought into the greenhouse, pit, cold frame, or cellar during the winter and forced. Rhubarb does not thrive in warm climates.

The use of rhubarb is principally during the early spring for making pies and sauces, and the stems may be canned for winter use.

### RUTA-BAGA.

The culture of the ruta-baga is the same as for the turnip, except that the former requires more room and a longer period for its growth. The roots are quite hardy and will withstand considerable frost. The ruta-baga is used like the turnip, and also for stock feed. Two pounds of seed are required for one acre.

### SALAD CHERVIL. (See CHERVIL.)

### SALSIFY, OR VEGETABLE OYSTER.

Sow seeds of salsify during the spring in the same manner as for parsnips or carrots. At the South, a sowing may be made in summer to produce roots for winter use. One ounce of seed is required to plant 100 feet of row, and on a large scale 10 pounds to the acre. After the plants are well established they should be thinned sufficiently to prevent their crowding. The cultivation should be the same as for parsnips or carrots, and frequent use of a wheel hoe will avoid the necessity for hand weeding. Salsify may be dug in the autumn and stored or allowed to remain in the ground during the winter, as its treatment is the same as for parsnips. Salsify is a biennial, and if the roots are not dug before the second season they will throw up stems and produce seed. It is of a weedy nature and care should be taken that it does not run wild by seeding freely.

Salsify is deserving of more general cultivation, as it is one of the more desirable of the root crops for the garden. The uses of salsify are similar to those of the parsnip, and when boiled and afterwards coated with rolled crackers and fried in butter it has a decided oyster flavor, from which the name vegetable oyster is derived.

### SCALLION. (See ONION.)

### SHALLOT. (See ONION.)

### SPINACH.

Spinach thrives in a rather cool climate and attains its best development in the Middle South, where it can be grown in the open ground during the winter. Large areas of spinach are grown near Norfolk, Va., cuttings being made at any time during the winter when the fields are not frozen or covered with snow. When the weather moderates in the early spring, the plants make a new growth, and a large crop of early greens is available. (Fig. 34.)

North of the latitude of Norfolk, spinach can be planted in the autumn and carried over winter by mulching with straw or leaves. Sow the seeds of spinach in drills 1 foot apart at the rate of 1 ounce to 100 feet of row, or 10 to 12 pounds to the acre. To produce good spinach, a rich loam which will give the plants a quick growth is required. As ordinarily grown, spinach occupies the land during the autumn and winter only and does not interfere with summer cultivation.

Spinach is an easily grown garden crop, and there is, perhaps, no other of its kind that will give as good satisfaction. Three or four ounces of seed, planted in the autumn after a summer crop has been harvested from the land, will produce an abundance of greens for the average family during the late autumn and early spring. In gathering spinach the entire plant is removed rather than merely cutting off the leaves. The larger plants are selected first, and the smaller or later ones are thus given room to develop. No thinning is required if this plan of harvesting is practiced.

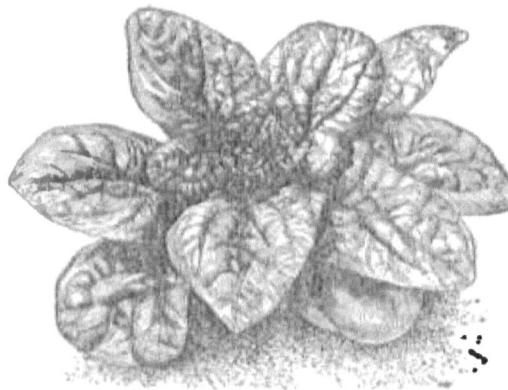

Fig. 34.—Spinach plant in proper condition for cutting.

### SQUASH.

There are two types of the squash, the bush varieties, which may be planted in hills 4 or 5 feet apart each way, and the running varieties, which will require from 8 to 16 feet for their development. Squashes may properly be grown in the garden, as 3 or 4 hills will produce all that are required for family use. They require practically the same soil and cultural methods as the muskmelon. A number of varieties are used during the summer in the same manner as vegetable marrow, but squashes are principally used during the winter, in much the same way as pumpkins, to which they are superior in many respects. Squashes are also used extensively for pie purposes. The varieties known as Hubbard and Boston Marrow are most commonly grown.

Squashes, like pumpkins, should be handled carefully to avoid bruising, and should be stored in a moderately warm but well ventilated room.

**SWEET POTATO. (See POTATO, SWEET.)**
**SWEET CORN. (See CORN, SWEET.)**
### TOMATO.

At the North it is very desirable to start tomato plants in a house or in a hotbed, and transplant once or twice in order to secure strong, vigorous plants by the time all danger from frost has passed. In the South the plants are started in cold frames or in beds in the open ground and protected by cotton cloth during the cool weather. In the southern parts of Florida and Texas large fields of tomatoes are planted in the same manner as corn, by placing five or six seeds in a hill where the plants are to be grown. After the seedlings become established, all but the two best are thinned out, and later but one is left in the hill.

The tomato is one of the crops that can be hastened to maturity by carefully growing the plants indoors and transplanting to the open ground. Pot-grown plants are especially desirable, and they may be brought to the blooming period by the time it is warm enough to safely plant them in the garden. If the plants are not to be trained but allowed to lie on the ground they should be set about 4 feet apart each way. If trimmed and tied to stakes they may be planted in rows 3 feet apart, and 18 inches apart in the row.

The tomato is one of the American vegetables that have come into general use during the past half century, and it now forms one of the most important of our garden crops. The uses of the tomato are too numerous and too well known to require attention here. For complete information regarding this vegetable, read Farmers' Bulletin No. 220, entitled "Tomatoes."

### TOP ONION. (See ONION.)
### TREE ONION. (See ONION.)
### TURNIP.

The turnip requires a rich soil, and may be grown either as an early or a late crop. For an early crop, sow the seeds in drills 12 to 18 inches apart as early in the spring as the condition of the soil will permit. Two pounds of seed are required to plant an acre. After the plants appear, thin to about 3 inches. The roots will be ready for use before hot weather. For late turnips the seeds are usually sown broadcast on land from which some early crop has been removed, generally during July or August, but later in the South. Turnips are quite hardy and the roots need not be gathered until after several frosts. Turnips may be stored in a cellar or buried in a pit outside. Before storing, the tops should be removed.

Turnips are used in pot-boiled preparations with potatoes, cabbage, and meat, or are boiled with pork, or mashed like potatoes.

### TURNIP-ROOTED CHERVIL. (See CHERVIL.)
### VEGETABLE MARROW.

The so-called vegetable marrows are closely allied to the pumpkin, both as to species and habit of growth, the principal difference being that the vegetable marrows are used while quite young and tender, and may be baked and served very much the same as sweet potatoes. The vegetable marrows should receive thorough cultivation in order that a tender product may be secured, and should be gathered while the outside skin is still so tender that it may easily be broken by the finger nail. The flesh is either boiled and mashed or baked in the oven and served with butter while hot.

### VEGETABLE OYSTER. (See SALSIFY.)
### WATER CRESS. (See CRESS.)
### WATERMELON. (See MELON—WATERMELON.)
### WELSH ONION. (See ONION.)
### WITLOOF. (See CHICORY.)

# GARDENER'S PLANTING TABLE.

*Quantity of seeds or number of plants required for a row 100 feet in length, with distances to plant, times for planting, and period required for production of crop.*

Brackets indicate that a late or second crop may be planted the same season.

| Kind of vegetable. | Seeds or plants required for 100 feet of row. | Distance for plants to stand— Rows apart. Horse cultivation. | Distance for plants to stand— Rows apart. Hand cultivation. | Distance for plants to stand— Plants apart in rows. | Depth of planting. | Time of planting in open ground. South. | Time of planting in open ground. North. | Ready for use after planting. |
|---|---|---|---|---|---|---|---|---|
| Artichoke, Globe | ¼ ounce | 3 to 4 ft | 2 to 3 ft | 2 to 3 ft | 1 to 2 in | Spring | Early spring | 15 months. |
| Artichoke, Jerusalem | 2 qts. tubers | 3 to 4 ft | 1 to 2 ft | 1 to 2 ft | 2 to 3 in | Spring | Early spring | 6 to 8 months. |
| Asparagus, seed | 1 ounce | 30 to 36 in | 1 to 2 ft | 3 to 5 in | 1 to 2 in | Autumn or early spring | Early spring | 3 to 4 years. |
| Asparagus, plants | 60 to 80 plants | 3 to 5 ft | 12 to 24 in | 15 to 20 in | 3 to 5 in | Autumn or early spring | Early spring | 1 to 3 years. |
| Beans, bush | 1 pint | 30 to 36 in | 18 to 24 in | 5 or 8 to ft | ½ to 2 in | February to April. [August to September.] | April to July | 40 to 65 days. |
| Beans, pole | ½ pint | 3 to 4 ft | 3 to 4 ft | 3 to 4 ft | 1 to 2 in | Late spring | May and June | 50 to 80 days. |
| Beets | 2 ounces | 24 to 36 in | 12 to 18 in | 5 or 6 to ft | 1 to 2 in | February to April. [August to September.] | April to August | 60 to 80 days. |
| Brussels sprouts | ¼ ounce | 30 to 36 in | 24 to 30 in | 16 to 24 in | ½ in | January to July | May and June | 90 to 120 days. |
| Cabbage, early | ¼ ounce | 30 to 36 in | 24 to 30 in | 12 to 18 in | ½ in | October to December | March and April. (Start in hotbed during February.) | 90 to 130 days. |
| Cabbage, late | ¼ ounce | 30 to 40 in | 24 to 36 in | 16 to 24 in | ½ in | June and July | May and June | 90 to 130 days. |
| Cardoon | ¼ ounce | 3 ft | 2 ft | 12 to 18 in | 1 to 2 in | Early spring | April and May | 5 to 6 months. |
| Carrot | 1 ounce | 30 to 36 in | 18 to 24 in | 6 or 7 to ft | ½ in | March and April. [September.] | April to June | 75 to 110 days. |
| Cauliflower | ¼ ounce | 30 to 36 in | 24 to 30 in | 14 to 18 in | ½ in | January and February. [June.] | April to June. (Start in hotbed during February or March.) | 100 to 130 days. |
| Celeriac | ¼ ounce | 30 to 36 in | 18 to 24 in | 4 or 5 to ft | ½ in | Late spring | May and June. (Start in cold frame during April.) | 100 to 150 days. |
| Celery | ¼ ounce | 3 to 6 ft | 18 to 36 in | 4 to 8 in | ½ in | August to October | May and June. (Start in hotbed or cold frame during March or April.) | 120 to 150 days. |
| Chervil | 1 ounce | 30 to 36 in | 18 to 24 in | 3 or 4 to ft | 1 in | Autumn | Autumn | 1 year. |
| Chicory | ¼ ounce | 30 to 36 in | 18 to 24 in | 4 or 5 to ft | ½ in | March and April | May and June | 5 to 6 months. |
| Citron | 1 ounce | 8 to 10 ft | 8 to 10 ft | 8 to 10 ft | 1 to 2 in | March and April | May and June | 100 to 130 days. |
| Collards | ¼ ounce | 30 to 36 in | 24 to 30 in | 14 to 18 in | ½ in | May and June | Late spring | 100 to 120 days. |
| Corn salad | 2 ounces | 30 in | 12 to 18 in | 5 or 6 to ft | ½ to 1 in | January and February. [September and October.] | March to September | 60 days. |
| Corn, sweet | ½ pint | 36 to 42 in | 30 to 36 in | 30 to 36 in | 1 to 2 in | February to April | May to July | 60 to 100 days. |
| Cress, upland | ¼ ounce | 30 in | 12 to 18 in | 4 or 5 to ft | ½ to 1 in | January and February. [Autumn.] | March to May. [September] | 30 to 40 days. |
| Cress, water | ¼ ounce | Broadcast | | | On surface | Early spring | April to September | 60 to 70 days. |
| Cucumber | ¼ ounce | 4 to 6 ft | 4 to 6 ft | 4 to 6 ft | 1 to 2 in | February and March. [September.] | April to July | 60 to 80 days. |
| Dandelion | ¼ ounce | 30 in | 18 to 24 in | 8 to 12 in | ½ in | Early spring or autumn | Early spring | 6 to 12 months. |